D1582858

THE MURKY CLOAK

". . . throw off the murky cloak of silence"

Rt.Hon. Anthony Greenwood, M.P., Minister of Housing and Local Government, 15th February, 1969

Contents

Preface

This is a partisan book. Although I have endeavoured in the following chapters to present both sides of the argument there is no doubt in my mind that the Press should be entitled, as of right, to attend all meetings of the great majority of local authority committees and sub-committees. Any exceptions, whether 'in the public interest' or whatever, should be capable of being fully and publicly justified. What has appalled me in the course of my service as a councillor on a large borough council and then on an even larger London borough council, and subsequently as a local government journalist, is the arrogance of a substantial number of elected representatives who apparently feel that once elected they are no longer responsible to or answerable to their public. Mrs. Barbara Castle has put her finger on it: 'The tendency is always for the public to be told too little, not too much, because, by their very nature, executives tend to be secretive.'

The subject is not a new one. This book could, and, perhaps, should, have been written ten, twenty, even fifty years ago but now with the quickening trend in local government affairs to even greater remoteness the need for better local authority-Press relations is all the more urgent. At present there are in England, Scotland and Wales over 9,000 local authorities of thirteen different types, each administering widely differing powers. As the result of the Reports of the Royal Commissions on Local Government in England and Scotland, and the various enquiries into local government in Wales, it has been proposed that (excluding existing parish councils on the one hand and the newly proposed 'local councils' or 'common councils' on the other) some 1,855 local authorities be replaced by 178 new-style councils. Indeed, following the further review of Welsh local government within the last few months the latter figure is likely to be even lower. The recently elected Government is not committed to these proposals but will, undoubtedly, propose a substantial reduction in the total number of councils.

A series of major reports on the staffing of local authorities, the structure of the welfare services and the national health service, and the need for public participation in planning and other services have emphasised that for many months now local government has been in a state of flux. Out of the melting-pot, however, is emerging the pattern for the future.

From all directions and for a variety of reasons – many of them admittedly good reasons – the trend is towards bigger and more powerful local authorities with greater financial resources and self-sufficient in a way that is, for most parts of the country, entirely new.

As local authorities grow in size and power there is a very real danger – a danger recognised by all concerned – that without adequate safeguards local government will become more remote. A number of remedies against this remoteness have been proposed by the Royal Commissions, the Government, the local authority associations and others. It is to be hoped that these remedies will have the desired effect but whether they do or not there remains one safeguard – the concern of this book – the Press.

Given adequate co-operation and facilities by local authorities the Press, local and national, could do much to reduce this remoteness to a minimum.

If this little book has even a marginal effect in checking the flight to cosy secrecy it will have succeeded.

Structure

The following chapters give examples of particular local authority-Press relationships, including a complete case history of one council's travail and detail the progress of the existing legislation as well as giving some tentative guidelines to the future state of relations between councils and their local newspapers in particular.

A series of Appendices give the source material upon which the book is based including the relevant statutes, Mr. Henry Brooke's famous circular and extracts from the research surveys conducted for the Maud Committee and for the Royal Commission on Local Government in England

My thanks are due to Charles Arnold-Baker, Secretary, National Association of Parish Councils; Mrs. Ann Carlton, Labour Party Local Government Officer; David Deeley, Liberal Party Local Government Officer; Laurence Evans, M.I.P.R., Local Government Information Officer; R.F. Farmer, F.C.C.S., General Secretary, Institute of Journalists; Councillor Major Henry Haydon, Chairman, National Union of Ratepayers' Associations; C. Gordon Page, Assistant Secretary, Newspaper Society; Noel S. Paul, Secretary, Press Council; and, officers of the Association of Municipal Corporations, the County Councils Association, the Rural District Councils Association, the Urban District Councils Association and the National Union of Journalists, all of whom helped me, answered my irritating questions, showed me their files and generally assisted me in spite of the pressures under which they work. My thanks are also due to Ray Jones, Editor, *Bexleyheath and Welling Observer* with whom I have discussed this problem over the years and who helped me to crystallise my thoughts; and to Mrs. Gwenllian Parrish, Features Editor, *Kentish Independent* who published my first efforts on this subject.

Mrs. Vera Flanagan read my miniscule writing and translated it into some elegant typescript and my wife, Bobby, castigated, cajoled and cossetted me at the appropriate moments. Finally, my thanks to the publishers Charles Knight who put up with my whims.

Acknowledgements are due to the following who kindly gave permission to reproduce extracts of material previously published elsewhere: The Editors of *Local Government Chronicle* and *Municipal Review*, the Editor of and correspondents to *The Times*; Charles Arnold-Baker; the A.M.C.; the U.D.C.A.; the L.G.I.O.; the Press Council; and the Controller of H.M. Stationery Office.

Introduction

Speaking at the Annual Dinner of the Rhondda East Constituency Labour Party at Porth, Glamorgan, on 8th January 1969, the Rt. Hon. Fred Peart, M.P., the then Lord President of the Council and Leader of the House of Commons, drew the attention of his audience to the essential need for a free press:

> 'Freedom of press and broadcasting has always been important in the development of a free society. Nowadays, however, it is even more important. The increasing complexity of modern society means that we are increasingly ruled by experts and specialists. This is inevitable, no matter who forms the government.
>
> In these circumstances, it is important that we should strengthen the checks on the experts. In a democracy, I firmly believe that the prime check must rest with elected representatives in local government and parliament. As for local democracy, we have begun to help in its revival by setting up the Maud Commission. The local press and local radio have an undoubted and important role to play in educating public opinion about local democracy.'

At the time that Mr. Peart was speaking the Report of the Maud Committee on the Management of Local Government[1] had been published for nearly two years, the White Paper on local government in Wales[2] was nearly as old and the Reports of the Royal Commissions on Local Government in England[3] and Scotland[4] were eagerly and, perhaps, apprehensively awaited.

A month later delegates to the Labour Party's Local Government Conference proved themselves less concerned with the freedom of the press to report on local government affairs than with the more fundamental problem whether, in the future, there would be local authorities of the traditional kind on which the press might report.

Since then the Royal Commissions have reported and the Labour Government has published its White Paper[5] on reform in England. The Royal Commission on Local Government in England recommended 58 'unitary' authorities and 3 metropolitan authorities in place of the conglomeration of existing authorities. The White Paper suggested marginal adjustments to these recommendations, proposing 51 'unitary' authorities and two additional metropolitan areas, making five in all. Greater London was specifically excluded from the scope of the Royal Commission, having been the subject of the Herbert Report[6] and the London Government Act, 1963.[7]

The result of all these proposals has meant, in the opinion of many people, the withdrawal of local government administration even further from the experience of the man in the street. In spite of a sharp reproof in the White Paper to 'some cynics and managerialists'[8] the proposals for 'local councils' devoid of any real or effective powers are widely regarded as an indication of the increasing remoteness of the new authorities now proposed. The experience in Greater London since its reorganisation in 1965 would seem to bear this out.

There is, thus, an even greater need now than when the Lord President of the Council was speaking for proper and effective communication by local authorities and a resulting greater co-operation between councils and the press. It is this effective communication that is the concern of this book – what has happened, what is happening today and what might be done to make communication between councils and their press even more effective in the light of the reforms now sweeping local government.

The proposals made in Chapter 16 are modest enough but if adopted they might well have a far-reaching effect on the public's attitude to local government and, equally, and in some ways even more importantly, on the attitude of councils to their public. If every effort is not made to improve this communication and the public loses confidence in local government then, as Mr. Greenwood said,[9] the local authorities 'will have only themselves to blame.'

1. Report of the Committee on Management in Local Government. March 1967.

2. Local Government in Wales. Cmnd. 3340. July 1967.

3. Royal Commission on Local Government in England. Cmnd. 4040. June 1969.

4. Royal Commission on Local Government in Scotland. Cmnd. 4150. September 1969.

5. Reform of Local Government in England. Cmnd. 4276. February 1970.

6. Royal Commission on Local Government in Greater London, 1957-60. Cmnd. 1164. October 1960.

7. London Government Act 1963. Eliz. 2. c.33.

8. Reform of Local Government in England, para. 57.

9. To the Labour Party Local Government Conference at Harrogate. 15th February 1969.

1 Without Comment

On 2nd December, 1965, the *Bolton Evening News* reported that 'within the circulation area of the *Evening News* and its associated weekly journals there are over twenty local authorities. Their attitudes towards the Press range from hostility, as at Turton and Hindley, through indifference to indulgent co-operation.'

On 25th May, 1966, a leader in the *Yorkshire Evening Press* congratulated Pocklington R.D.C. on admitting the Press to committees.

Leamington Spa Courier chided Leamington Council for non-admission (15th July, 1966).

'Open it up' commanded the *Daily Mail* in an editorial on 1st June, 1966.

On 4th November, 1966, the *Bucks Free Press* reported that Chalfont St. Peter Parish Council had asked Amersham R.D.C. to open up committees.

The *Western Daily Press,* Bristol, had a go at two local authorities in its editorial on 24th November, 1966 – firstly against Cirencester R.D.C. which excluded the Press during the discussion of the auditor's report which criticised the Council for allowing £7,000 of rate arrears to accumulate and, secondly, against Bath Borough Council which debated the controversial Kelston Park proposals in private.

'Councillor Palethorpe lunges at Press again', stated the headline in the *Walthamstow Guardian* of 2nd December, 1966, over a story of accusations of inaccurate reporting; reporters who know nothing about local government; and, a 'witch-hunt' organised by members of the NUJ.

The *Leamington Spa Courier*, 2nd December, 1966,

reported that Southam councillors had been told not to speak to the Press until committee recommendations had been approved at the Council meeting.

On the same day it was reported that Millom R.D.C. voted 9-8 for admitting the Press to the Health Committee meeting (*Barrow News*).

Peterborough Advertiser wanted to know why Huntingdon and Godmanchester Borough Council had excluded the paper from a debate on trading from council houses (2nd December, 1966).

The Ashford Local Labour Party complained to Ashford Council about its practice of sending reports to the Press before Council meetings as this 'lead to poor reporting of the meetings'. (*Kentish Express,* 9th December, 1966).

Cambridge News of 27th January, 1967, carried an article by Mr. Eric Lubbock, M.P. entitled 'Publicity Best Ombudsman'.

Gainsborough U.D.C. defeated a notion to admit the Press to committee by 17-5 in spite of a statement that 'too much Council business is conducted in secret.' (*Retford, Gainsborough and Worksop Times*).

The *Western Daily Press*, Bristol, reported that Liberals had suggested to Wells City Council that committees should be opened up (20th February, 1967).

In a very critical article the *St. Ives Times* attacked St. Ives Borough Council for refusing to admit the Press to committees (24th February, 1967).

The exclusion of the Press from a Redcar Council committee 'for the first time in many years' while discussion took place on a letter from an official regarding his terms of employment was reported by the *Middlesborough Evening Gazette* on 24th February, 1967.

The *Wiltshire Gazette* on 2nd March, 1967, noted a policy change by Berkshire County Council, nine more committees would be open to the Press although the planning committee would stay closed.

On 13th April, 1967, the *Oxford Mail* reported complaints by councillors on Bullingdon R.D.C. that committee recommendations were being commented on by the paper before they were approved by the Council meeting.

'Debate public matters openly' stated a headline in the

Bingley and Shipley Guardian on 21st April, 1967.

'Two new councils – the North Shropshire R.D.C. and the enlarged Oswestry R.D.C. – have, regrettably in our view, joined the ranks of those not prepared to let the Press attend their committee meetings,' reported the *Shropshire Star* on 26th April, 1967.

On 5th May, 1967, the *Aldershot News* commented, 'Aldershot Council's 'sealed-lips brigade' won another victory when with a majority of three they voted not to admit the Press to meetings of the housing committee'.

The *Truro West Briton* reported on 25th May, 1967, that a move to ban the Press from Truro City redevelopment committee discussions 'failed dismally'.

Continued exclusion of the Press by Reading Council was described in the Reading *Evening Post* of 15th June, 1967, as 'Reading's sad decision.'

On 28th June, 1967, the *Oxford Mail* was criticising another local authority: 'Woodstock Borough Council is wrong to decide to hold its committee meetings in secret, to refuse to allow the public or the Press into them – and to muzzle its committee chairmen as well.'

An attempt by Councillor Wallace Lawler (Lib.), later M.P. for Birmingham, Ladywood, to persuade Birmingham City Council to adopt an 'open-door policy' failed, according to the *Birmingham Evening Mail and Despatch* of 19th July, 1967, when only two members voted in favour. It was said in debate by a Labour member that it would be the 'height of absurdity to suggest that democracy would suffer if the Press is not admitted to Council committee meetings' and by a Conservative member that 'It would be a disadvantage to have the Press present when an important and serious subject was under discussion."

'Admit Press to Herefordshire County Council committee meetings and dispel public doubt' – headline in *Hereford Evening News*, 25th July, 1967.

On 28th July, 1967, the *Cambridge Daily News* reported that Cambridge Council had rejected a motion to admit the Press to committee meetings by 23-9.

Slough Observer reported 'Eton Rural will keep the door closed' (28th July, 1967).

On 7th November, 1967, the *Yorkshire Evening Post*

reported that the Yorkshire County Council had decided to give a six months' trial to admitting the Press to committee meetings.

North Walsham U.D.C. agreed to admit the press to all committees stated the *Eastern Evening News* on 1st February, 1968.

In March, 1968, the *Sutton and Cheam Herald* carried the headline 'Ban on Press and Public – 'Negation of Democracy'.'

Hampstead News reported on 13th February, 1970, that Labour councillors would urge Camden Council to admit the Press to committee 'subject to certain conditions'.

Islington Council admits the Press 'to all but the policy committee' and Hackney to all committees 'but administration'. (*Islington Guardian*)

The former leader of Exeter Labour Group called for admission of the Press to Plymouth City Council's committee meetings in the *Western Evening Herald* of 26th February, 1970.

The *Birmingham Post* reported, on 25th February, 1970, that Lichfield City Council Parks and Recreation Committee would be open to the Press 'with reservations.' Reporters can only record the recommendations of the meetings – not the speeches of the councillors – and they will not receive copies of reports prepared by Council officers.

Derby Town Council debated the admission of the Press to committees, according to the *Derbyshire Advertiser* of 6th March, 1970, but on a straight vote between the majority Conservative group and the Labour group the motion was defeated. The Chairman of the Council's education committee suggested that the proposal was not sincere but put forward because of 'base political motives.'

2 What happened in Tenby

If Frank Britten Mason had brushed up a little more on his shorthand the present relationship between the press and local authorities might well have been very different.

In 1907 Mr. Mason, the proprietor of the *Tenby Observer*, had written a report of a meeting of Tenby Borough Council which had displeased the members. That in itself was not, and is not, an unusual happening either in Tenby or anywhere else in Britain. But what happened next had far-reaching effects.

In 1895 the Corporation had passed a resolution permitting the representatives of newspapers to attend their meetings, subject to the right of the council to exclude them on 'necessary occasions', but as a result of the irritating report the councillors, smarting from their injured pride, decided that they had had enough of Mr. Mason. They passed a resolution that he 'be informed that he will not be permitted to attend again personally as reporter to his own paper until he proves himself to the satisfaction of the council to be an efficient shorthand writer.' The council, adding salt to Mr. Mason's wounds, did not refuse permission to his usual shorthand reporter to attend.

But Mr. Mason was made of stern stuff. In March, 1907, he attended a council meeting, of which notice had been sent to his newspaper's office, and he refused to leave when requested by the mayor. As he threatened to repeat the performance at subsequent meetings the council decided to meet his challenge head-on and brought an action in the Chancery Division claiming a declaration that they had the right to exclude all persons who were not members of the council from the meetings of the council or meetings of the committees of the council, and also seeking an injunction restraining Mr. Mason from trespassing on their property; from entering the council chamber during meetings; and from being present at meetings without their permission.

Mr. Mason's defence was three-pronged. He claimed the right to attend firstly, as a burgess of the borough, that is, as an inhabitant with full municipal rights; secondly, as a representative of a newspaper (the *Tenby Observer*); and finally, as a member of the public at what he claimed were public meetings.

The case was heard in November, 1907 before a desperately ill Mr. Justice Kekewich who in this case prepared but did not personally deliver his last judgment. The case for the council was simple in the extreme – the business of the meeting could not be conducted properly if the public were admitted, and if every ratepayer attended it would be wholly impossible. The Municipal Corporations Act, 1882 governed these meetings but the Act said nothing about the admission of the public or reporters.

Burgesses could see the council minutes but were not entitled to committee minutes. The claim to attend as a member of the public said Mr. Lawrence K.C., for the council, was 'absurd'. There was no decision on the point.

The defence was that the council, having made a standing order to admit reporters, could not then exclude a particular member of the Press. The meetings of the council were public meetings and it was not necessary to hold them in private. At the time of the case the public was admitted to parish meetings under the Local Government Act, 1894, and an attempt was made to draw a parallel between the parish and the borough. If, said, Mr. Jessel K.C., no admission was to be allowed why was the public informed of the meeting?

Mr. Justice Kekewich took a week to consider his verdict and because of his serious illness his judgment was read by Mr. Justice Parker. In spite of his infirmity his judgment lost nothing in clarity or logic. He was quite firm – a council can make and unmake standing orders and however binding they are on the council they cannot confer rights on strangers. The notice given to the newspaper was for convenience only. The only arguable point thought Mr.

Justice Kekewich, having disposed of a number of minor points, was the claim that the meetings were public meetings. But, he said, they were dealing with 'the creature of statute' and there was no room for the application of the common law.

There was no expression of any right of attendance in the Municipal Corporations Act, 1882 and the judge did not think it could be inferred. He found in favour of Tenby Corporation and gave them their injunction.

Mr. Mason appealed and his case was cogently restated, emphasis being placed on the grounds of public policy that matters of great public interest should be public. The Master of the Rolls was not swayed by this or any of the other earlier stated arguments. Mr. Justice Kekewich's judgment could not be faulted. 'I desire to say,' said Cozens-Hardy, M.R., 'that I agree with every word of that judgment; and I should be quite content to adopt it without adding any remarks of my own.'

Nevertheless, as is the wont of lawyers, he did deliver his own judgment which reinforced the right of Tenby Council to exclude Mr. Mason from its deliberations. His colleagues on the bench of the Court of Appeal, Lords Justices Fletcher Moulton and Buckley concurred and Mr. Mason's appeal was dismissed, unfortunately for him, with costs.

In spite of the cut-and-dried nature of the two judgments there was an undercurrent in the proceedings that all was not well. Certainly there was public feeling that there *should* be a right of admission of the general public to local authority (and other public authority) meetings. Indeed, many people including a number of politicians had been surprised by the revelation during the court hearings that there was no right in common law to such admission.

Arthur Henderson, M.P., later to be Leader of the Parliamentary Labour Party and a one-time member of the Newcastle City Council, Durham County Council and ex-Mayor of Darlington, introduced the Local Authorities (Admission of the Press to Meetings) Bill into the House of Commons. The Bill, whose short title is self-explanatory, sought to give Mr. Mason and any other of his journalist colleagues the right to attend the meetings of a local authority. The Bill was widely supported and enacted on 21st

December, 1908. The Act is reproduced in full in Appendix I, p. 100.

It is interesting to note that the Act applied not only to local authorities in the presently accepted sense but also to education committees,[1] boards of guardians and joint committees,[2] a central body and a distress committee under the Unemployed Workmen Act, 1905, the Metropolitan Water Board and any other local body with the power to make a rate.

Most of these other bodies have subsequently disappeared but from 1908 to 1960 Mr. Henderson's Act was to govern proceedings between local authorities and the Press.

1. Established under the Education Act, 1902.
2. Constituted in pursuance of s.8 of the Poor Law Act, 1879.

3 Mrs Thatcher's Bill

During the 1920s and 1930s the provisions of the 1908 Act became increasingly less satisfactory as the bodies specified in the enactment gradually disappeared, but apart from one short-lived effort in 1930 little effort was made to remedy the situation and the war then intervened, effectively postponing attempts at reform.

On 28th January, 1949, Mr. Robert Grimston (Con., Westbury) introduced his Public Bodies (Admission of Press) Bill supported by, among others. Messrs. Beswick and Byers (now Lords Beswick and Byers). The Bill was quite straightforward – its chief clause called for the admission of 'representatives of the press' to the meetings of bodies specified in the schedule to the Bill, but provided that a majority vote at the particular meeting could exclude the press 'in the public interest'. The Bill's schedule included committees of local authorities consisting of all members of the authority, education committees, various consultative councils, regional hospital boards, river boards and food control committees. In spite of all-party support this Bill made no progress.

Seven years later, on 1st August, 1956, another Conservative M.P., Mr. J.E.S. Simon (Middlesborough West) introduced another Private Member's Bill supported by the prime mover of the previous Bill, now Sir Robert Grimston; Labour M.P.s, Sir Leslie Plummer, Mr. Wedgwood Benn and Mr. Donnelly; Conservatives, Sir Lionel Heald, Mr. Fletcher-Cooke and Miss (now Dame) Joan Vickers; and Liberal, Mr. Jo Grimond. This Bill, the Public Bodies (Admission of the Press to Meetings) Bill, was rather more complex than its predecessor. The types of public body to which the press should be admitted were extended to no less than twenty-seven and there were provisions for the supply of documents to the press while the exceptions to the provisions were made more comprehensive. This Bill was, nevertheless, no more successful than that of 1949.

In 1959 a printing strike was exacerbated when a number of Labour-controlled councils excluded from their meetings 'blackleg' reporters working for newspapers which continued publication during the strike. The Conservative Government threatened strong action against any such further reprisals as being 'wholly contrary to the spirit of the existing law' and disquiet was felt in all quarters of local government.

Finally on 11th November, 1959, the Public Bodies (Admission of the Press to Meetings) Bill was presented in the House of Commons by Mrs. Margaret Thatcher, (Con., Finchley). Her co-sponsors were Conservatives, Sir Lionel Heald, Sir Robert Grimston, Sir Peter Agnew, Wing-Commander Grant Ferris and Messrs. Corfield, Bishop, Kirk, Hobson and Gurden. Sir Robert Grimston had been a sponsor of both previous Bills and Sir Lionel Heald and Mr. Kirk had been sponsors of the 1956 Bill. The second reading of the Bill was quite a Parliamentary occasion. Vivacious Mrs. Thatcher,[1] aged 35, had been elected to Parliament on 8th October, 1959, just one month before she presented her Bill and when she rose to speak on the second reading she had not spoken before in the House. In other words, in her maiden speech Mrs. Thatcher was presenting an important Private Member's Bill which obtained that all important ingredient from the Government, namely Parliamentary time.

Doubtless her training as a barrister specialising in taxation matters helped her, but it is significant that she was congratulated by other Members on both sides of the House for her lucid presentation of the Bill 'with hardly a reference to notes'.

The Bill was a further improvement on the 1956 version and seemed, in its original form, a very much more workmanlike document. The Bill as it was finally enacted is to be found in Appendix 2, p.102, but in its original form two additional types of body to which it should apply were included in the accompanying schedule. These were watch committees and other police authority bodies and probation committees. Both were removed during the committee stage.

The Bill struck trouble within the first hour of debate when it was found that the sponsors wished to include provisions to admit other members of the public, apart from the Press, to meetings of local authorities, but owing to a technicality the 'short title' of the Bill seemed to preclude any such extension of its powers. One of those esoteric Parliamentary arguments on procedure developed but common sense prevailed and the title was altered during the committee stage to embrace the sponsors' wishes, becoming the Public Bodies (Admission to Meetings) Bill.

Presenting the Bill[2] Mrs. Thatcher specified its object, as had Mr. Henderson when introducing the 1908 Bill, as that of, 'guarding the rights of members of the public by enabling the fullest information to be obtained for them in regard to the actions of their representatives upon local authorities'.

She thought that the public had a right to know what its elected representatives were doing not least because of the huge amount of money spent by local government. Mrs. Thatcher quoted a figure of £1,400 million expenditure in England and Wales. This figure has more than doubled in the ten years since the debate. Publicity, she averred, was a check against arbitary action and stimulated public interest. Of course, she said, a certain amount of discussion ought to be in private and her Bill made provision for this.

Detailing the history of her measure she pointed out that as long ago as 1930 the then Labour Member for South Shields, Mr. J.C. Ede, had introduced a Private Member's Bill, shortly after the Local Government Act, 1929 had abolished boards of guardians, one of the bodies to which the Press was admitted under the 1908 Act. The Bill had failed in spite of a second reading because of a change of Government. The provisions of the Local Government Act, 1933 had only worsened the position by allowing councils to resolve themselves into committee merely to exclude the Press, whether or not that exclusion was justified by the nature of the business under discussion.

Her Bill specifically stated, in clause 9, that the powers would apply 'in relation to *any committee* of the body whose normal functions consist to a substantial extent of discharging functions of the body under powers delegated to the committee by the body as that section applies in relation to the body itself,' and Mrs. Thatcher drew attention to this in her speech. The fate of the clause at later stages was a sad one.

Turning to reasons for excluding the press Mrs. Thatcher said: 'I suggest most earnestly that when the press is excluded it must be because of some particular reason arising from the proceedings of the local authority at the time, and there must be very good reason for the exclusion.'

Mrs. Thatcher, perhaps realising the vagueness of her 'very good reason' was then more specific: 'The real reason for excluding the Press is that publicity of the matter to be discussed would be prejudicial to the public interest.'

There were, she thought, two main groups of reasons for exclusion. The first would concern confidential matters such as Government communications asking for local authority opinions before public discussion of a particular subject. The second might relate to staff matters, contracts, legal proceedings and the discussion of tenders.

Turning to the supply of council documents to the press, Mrs. Thatcher noted, 'the very wide variation in practice between the number of documents which different local authorities give to the press.'

The Bill, therefore, provided for a copy of the agenda of a meeting to be supplied to the Press on request, and if necessary on payment of postage, together with any further documents or particulars necessary to indicate the nature of the items included or even copies of reports supplied to members of the authorities. Mrs. Thatcher and her co-sponsors would not countenance any extension of the qualified privilege for elected members of local authorities but a consequential provision ensured that just because the Press was present that qualified privilege should not cease to exist.

Mr. Frederick Corfield (Con., Gloucestershire, South), seconding the Bill's second reading, had scarcely finished congratulating Mrs. Thatcher when he was in trouble over the 'short title' problems mentioned earlier (p.11). Having weathered the storm he returned to his central theme:

'... it is not the purpose of the Bill to confer privileges on the Press as such. The purpose of the Bill is to ensure to the Press, as the natural channel between electors and elected, the facilities necessary for the Press to fulfil that function.'

Answering an argument heard both before the publication of the Bill and since he said,

'It is perfectly true that in central government administrative decisions are taken within the walls of a Government Department, but nevertheless they are taken in the name of a responsible Minister who can be questioned in this House and can be required to justify those decisions on the floor of the House. That seems to me to be an absolutely basic safeguard to our liberties. But as these decisions become delegated to local authorities, ministerial responsibility must be correspondingly weakened and in some cases abrogated altogether. In that case, the private citizen is deprived of the right to that last final appeal to this House through his Parliamentary representative.'

Mr. Corfield thought that the only substitute was that decisions should be announced in public after due notice in public and in conditions which permit public discussion.

He was concerned that the position of local government officers should not be jeopardised but he thought that there was a great deal of purely factual information that officers could just as well give to the local press as to members of the council.

1. Now the Secretary of State for Education and Science and described by Andrew Roth in *The M.P.'s Chart* as 'Intelligent, charming; strong will'.

2. H.C. Debates, 5th February, 1960, Vol.616, cols. 1350–1454.

4 Mrs Thatcher's Bill – The Debate

The first signs of opposition came from the late Mr. Gerry Reynolds (Lab., Islington, North) who was both an Alderman and, at one time, the Labour Party's Local Government Officer. He moved an amendment declining to give the Bill a second reading. The wording is significant as it enshrines many of the arguments put forward by opponents of opening up committees: 'This House, while believing that good relationships between the Press and public bodies can only be achieved through greater understanding, tolerance and good sense on behalf of the parties concerned, and anxious that all public bodies should assist the press as much as possible in the exercise of its proper functions, declines to give a Second Reading to a Bill which would disrupt satisfactory arrangements which already exist in many parts of the country.' He agreed that local authorities must give maximum assistance to the press but he felt that,

'The exceptions and provisions in the Bill will, in many parts of the country, probably lead to greater animosity between the pub lic bodies and the press rather than ease the relationship between them.'

Mr. Reynolds thought that the resolution calling for exclusion of the press on the grounds of public interest would be passed on 'dozens of occasions every year' and this would, inevitably, lead to friction and headlines about 'gags' and 'under-cover work'. He declared that the financial argument put forward by Mrs. Thatcher was a false one as most of the money spent by local authorities was, in fact, under the control of central government departments who were already answerable through Parliament.

'To argue,' said Mr. Reynolds, 'that the Press should be permitted to attend the committee meetings of local authorities in order to make sure that people generally are informed of what is done by the council is, I think, to be derogatory to the many members of local authorities who are in a minority party or group. It is apparently suggested that they are not capable of bringing to the notice of the electorate and the Press at public council meetings anything which they regard as wrongly done in a closed committee meeting of the council.'

On the question of unwelcome publicity, Mr. Reynolds was of the opinion that the knowledge that the Press would be at committee meetings might inhibit people from giving to the local authority the type of information which is often required from them in order to make the right decisions.

For instance, 'those asked to give references about people who apply to act as foster parents may be very hesitant because they will have at the back of their minds the thought, wrong though the idea may be, that there is a good chance of information they provide reaching the Press and becoming public.'

Mr. Reynolds was in favour of the House expressing its views and leaving it to the good sense of locally elected bodies to decide the detailed course of action which they would take.

Finally he was of the opinion that once the glare of the local Press was extended to committee meetings the party whip system would also extend into those committees:

'This Bill will lead to more back door methods of carrying out local authority work. The work would be driven from the committee into the hands of a few people meeting together in a little gang outside.'

Mr. Reynolds was supported by Mr. Arthur Skeffington (Lab., Hayes and Harlington), later Joint Parliamentary Secretary, Ministry of Housing and Local Government (see also chapter 13, 'People and Planning – the Skeffington Report').

'We all agree', he said, 'that the dissemination of information in the fullest form, at the earliest possible stage, is the only guarantee of good local government.'

His first objection to the Bill was that it proposed to

give a special privilege to representatives of a commercial organisation, the Press, while it was not proposed to give that privilege to the public. He thought that there were three types of practical problem not catered for in Mrs. Thatcher's measure. Firstly, there were some welfare cases where it would not be proper to publicise the harrowing details; secondly, certain children's committee deliberations would suffer from the presence of the Press. Thirdly, he thought that prosecutions undertaken by health committees would not benefit if the offences concerned could not be frankly discussed because of the presence of reporters. He thought that publicity might be most detrimental in the case of watch committees (which were subsequently removed from the schedule).

On planning cases, Mr. Skeffington declared that before town and country planning permission is given there is a good deal of investigation and discussion, and, 'if it is reported it must have a very considerable effect upon the price at which the land or other property is to be sold.' As a final suggestion, Mr. Skeffington proposed that there should be, 'a preparatory code of conduct which should be binding as far as possible both on the press and the local authorities.' (See chapter 13, p.77.)

Mr. Dudley Smith, (Con., Brentford and Chiswick)[1], now Under Secretary, Employment and Productivity, also in a maiden speech, supported the Bill unreservedly both as a professional journalist and as a member of the Middlesex County Council. Contrary to Mr. Skeffington he did not think that special privileges were being asked for by the press. In his view the press 'represents the public and on many occasions *is* the public.'

Mr. Smith felt that the fear that debate in committee might be exaggerated with the press present was itself exaggerated and that, 'after the first novelty of the measure had died down things will settle down well and there will be a great degree of co-operation between the Press and local government.'

Mrs. Barbara Castle (Lab., Blackburn), later First Secretary of State and Secretary of State for Employment and Productivity, also supported the Bill both as a journalist and as a former member of two local authorities. Hitting at the arrogance of some local authority members, she said, 'We tend to forget that just because we have been elected we do not thereby become someone special, someone who can disregard the claims to knowledge by the public who gave us our being and without whom we should not exist.'

Mr. Michael Stewart (Lab., Fulham), who became Secretary of State for Foreign and Commonwealth Affairs, gave a cautious welcome to the Bill, which he hoped to amend during its progress through Parliament. He was anxious to hear the Government's attitude, and he did not have long to wait. Mr. Henry Brooke (now Lord Brooke of Cumnor), the Minister of Housing and Local Government and Minister for Welsh Affairs, reminded the House that the Conservative manifesto prior to the 1959 election contained a pledge to ensure that the press would have proper facilities for reporting the proceedings of local authorities. As far as Mr. Brooke was concerned the pledge still stood and the Government intended to fulfil it. It had been his intention prior to the publication of Mrs. Thatcher's Bill to investigate a possible voluntary code of conduct. In the event his Ministry had done what it could to assist Mrs. Thatcher. He gave his support to the Bill, 'because though it is not exactly the method I should have chosen, it is a genuine and sincere endeavour to remedy a situation which is at present unsatisfactory.'

On a free vote with the whips off the Bill received a second reading by 152 votes to 39.

The Bill's progress through committee was one of emasculation. Some of the more controversial bodies were removed from the schedule, the references to the press were extended to include the public but, of most significance, the committee meetings to which the press and public could be admitted were restricted to those on which *all* members of the local authority serve. In one stroke this nullified a great deal of the good intentions of the Bill's sponsors. The amendment meant that a very large and convenient loophole now existed and within a matter of weeks of the Royal Assent, committees up and down the country were being quietly reshuffled and rejigged so that the provisions of the Act might not apply.

The feeling of M.P.s was, perhaps, best summed up by

Mr. Peter Kirk (Con., Gravesend): 'In many ways the Bill is a disappointment. I should have liked to see it much nearer to its original form, but politics, I suppose, is the art of the possible. The Bill certainly is an immense improvement on the existing law and for that reason it must be welcomed.'[2]

1. Mr. Smith is now the M.P. for Warwick and Leamington.
2. H.C. Debates. 13th May, 1960. Vol.623, col. 829.

5 The Local Authority Associations React

Following the enactment of the Public Bodies (Admission to Meetings) Act, 1960 advice and instructions were issued by the various local authority associations. The Urban District Councils Association, for example, issued in April, 1961 a 'Memorandum on Practical Points' which was designed to furnish information on a number of practical points arising from the Act. The UDCA was quick off the mark and its memorandum was issued before the Minister's circular, which is reproduced in Appendix 4, p.108.

Certain important points were clarified, such as the definition of the public who might be admitted to meetings. Attention was drawn to the Solicitor General's statement during the committee stage of the Bill[1] when he indicated that in his view 'public' meant members of the community generally. 'It is a fairly well understood term, and I think that it would be a mistake to try to define it in the context of this Bill. It certainly goes beyond ratepayers and residents. It extends, indeed, to members of the community generally.'

The UDCA pamphlet discussed the provision of accommodation for the press and the vexed question of the power of exclusion on grounds of prejudice to the public interest. It thought that staff matters – although not *all* staff matters – such as promotion, dismissals, reprimands, etc., were within the scope of the exclusion clause. General discussions on, for instance, a national pay award ought not to be held with the press excluded.

Mrs. Thatcher, in the course of the debate in Parliament, had voiced some doubts about councillors' qualified privilege and the UDCA sought counsel's opinion on the subject of the privilege attaching to documents supplied under the terms of the Act. According to the pamphlet:

> 'When a meeting is required to be open to the public, during the proceedings or any part of them a local authority must, under Section 1(4)(b), supply to any newspaper a copy of the agenda as supplied to members of the authority (subject to certain exclusions), together with such further statements or particulars, if any, as are necessary to indicate the nature of the items or if thought fit in the case of any item, with copies of any reports or other documents supplied to members of the local authority in connection with the item. In relation to those further statements there is the alternative of a separately prepared document or supply of copies of reports or other documents where such latter course is an effective and convenient way of supplying the information. The primary way of supplying the supplementary information is a separately prepared statement.
>
> 'Under Section 1(5) the agenda and any separately prepared document containing supplementary information *has the benefit of qualified privilege.* A copy of a report or other document issued to a newspaper in pursuance of the alternative way of supplying supplementary information does not attract qualified privilege.'

The Association of Municipal Corporations sent to its member corporations, on 21st June, 1961, a copy of the report of its general purposes committee[2] in which its own attitudes to the new legislation were detailed. As far back as 1946 the AMC had made recommendations which were not very different to the final form of Mrs. Thatcher's Act and hence the committee's report recommended that its members should make every effort to observe the law, 'not only in the letter but in the spirit.'

The essence of the democratic system of government, declared the AMC is that, 'there should be public discussion of all public matters and any device by means of committee procedure or otherwise which is designed to prevent discussion in public is strongly deprecated.'

Without waiting for argument the AMC anticipated one of the points that some councillors had advanced at the time of the passage of the Bill through Parliament:

'The extent of the business now done by local authorities creates a danger that its very volume may prevent public discussion of those things which must be done and which should be seen to be done and discussed in public. It is understandable that members of local councils may wish to avoid repetition of discussions which take place in a committee but there is no doubt that if the public is to be properly informed this, in fact, is necessary or some other means must be found of informing the press and the public.'

At least one authority appears to have taken this advice seriously, as Dr. Dilys Hill pointed out in an article in the *Local Government Chronicle,* 11th December, 1965. 'One council faced with this situation found that they could only rely on getting publicity for important topics by starting a row in council meetings.'

The AMC was concerned that the local press should co-operate with councils if for no other reason than that where the council does not feel that it has had 'a fair crack of the whip, there is more likely to be friction, lack of co-operation and demands to exclude the Press from the council's debates than is the case where there has been in the past a history of co-operation between the council and the Press, and of fair reporting of the council's acts.'

The Association was convinced, as it had made known to M.P.s during the passage of the Bill, that most of its members had satisfactory arrangements with the local press, and a rather weak little passage in the report let the councils off the hook:

'In drawing attention to the details mentioned below, the General Purposes Committee wish to record their belief that most members of the Association have satisfactory arrangements with the local press which operate to their mutual advantage. All of the practices recommended below are probably in operation in many areas. Where they are not, it will frequently be the case that some other equally convenient arrangements will have been worked out locally.'

Even on the most charitable interpretation of this passage the AMC was anxious not to offend its members. The results of recent surveys (see chapter 12) show an unsatisfactory situation today – how much worse it was in 1961 can only be guessed at. Nevertheless this should not detract from the very sound advice given in the Association's letter.

The right of exclusion concerned the AMC as it had the UDCA, and in justification of the right of exclusion its report paraphrased Mr. Alfred Wise, Conservative Member for Rugby, who in the course of the second reading debate on the Bill[3] had said: 'The House (of Commons) is a legislature. Local government is an administration. One cannot administer in a goldfish pond.'

'Local councils,' stated the AMC, 'unlike Parliament, are executive bodies and carry both the responsibility for policy decisions and the oversight of day-to-day administration.'

The Association thought that the personal details of individuals and their families ought not to be discussed in public and the press should be excluded for negotiations for the acquisition of land and the making of other contracts involving large sums of money, prosecutions and other proceedings.

Finally, the AMC was very concerned that only authorised officers or members should make contact with the local press: 'It is considered most undesirable that individual members of committees or officers not specifically authorised should make statements to reporters about what has happened in a committee. Usually such statements are contrary to standing orders.' For an opinion on these standing orders, see Charles Arnold-Baker's letter on p.25. It was felt that because a proper procedure had been established for giving information to the press on all important matters that alone should be sufficient to discourage reporters from trying to obtain unauthorised statements from members of committees.

While the advice given by the larger local authority associations was tempered with caution and a certain feeling of resentment that Parliament should have interfered in a province that belonged strictly to the town hall, the National Association of Parish Councils had no such reservations and in a succinct statement in the Parish Councils' 'bible', *New Law and Practice of Parish Administration*, the Secretary of the NAPC, Charles Arnold-Baker wrote:

'There is no authority for the commonly-held belief that proceedings of committees are confidential, but neither the press nor the public are entitled to be present at committees as of right. In few cases is there any good reason for excluding the press or the public from committee meetings and in fewer still is it necessary to impose secrecy upon the members.

'As a rule, however, it is desirable to treat the discussion of the following types of business as confidential:

(a) engagement, terms of service, conduct and dismissal of employees;
(b) terms of tenders, and proposals and counter-proposals in negotiation for contracts;
(c) preparation of cases in legal proceedings;
(d) the early stages of any dispute.'

1. Third sitting, 30th March 1960, col. 162.
2. Report 5/1961, 1st June, 1961.
3. H.C. Debates, 5th February 1960, Vol.616, col. 1407.

6 How the Thatcher Act Worked

It is generally agreed that Mrs. Thatcher's Bill as enacted was a very different creature from that first introduced in the Commons on 5th February, 1960. The most frequently used epithet, 'emasculated', was applied right from the start, as soon as it was evident that the Act would be a very much weaker measure than was originally intended. The watering down at the committee stage meant that the ills for which it was supposed to be the panacea would continue, and the Act has been the subject of criticism at regular intervals since it came onto the statute book.

A report[1] from the Midlands Correspondent of *The Times* sparked a critical editorial comment: 'The Public Bodies (Admission to Meetings) Act has now been in force for some eighteen months, and there is evidence to show that some small local authorities are ignoring the spirit, if not the letter, of the law.'[2]

Correspondents to *The Times* letters page were quick to agree. Frank Staniforth, the managing editor of North of England Newspapers Co. Ltd., wrote that the Act: 'has had little practical effect, except, as your Midlands Correspondent points out, to encourage some local authorities to reduce the membership of committees to dodge the legislation.'[3]

Roper Mead, a past president of the National Union of Journalists, wrote on the same day: 'If the recalcitrant authorities insist on continuing to regard local government as the exclusive preserve of a few elected and self-regarded infallibles it is time to think of new and stronger legislation to ensure that they fall into line.'

In view of the arguments that he and other correspondents had put forward he wanted to know what the new Minister, Sir Keith Joseph, was going to do. Sir Keith was silent, which was hardly surprising, as in 1960, during the passage of the Bill through Parliament, he was reported as addressing the Rural District Councils Association Conference in the following unambiguous terms:

'... a number of you who have committees of this kind (comprising all members of the council) may well think it right to alter their composition so that they no longer consist of all members of the council. I should like to assure you that there will be no criticism from the Minister that to do so would be an evasion of the Bill'.[4]

Sir Keith was then Parliamentary Secretary, Ministry of Housing and Local Government, under Mr. Henry Brooke and became the Minister on 13th July, 1962, succeeding Dr. Charles Hill who was in that office for only nine months.

In following days a number of correspondents revealed how particular authorities were evading their responsibilities:

'In Buckinghamshire the County Council not only refuses admission to meetings of its own committees and sub-committees but even brought pressure to bear on a town council which itself sought to implement the spirit of the Act by admitting members of the public to its own planning meetings.'[5]

'The Middlesex County Council only publishes those few items reported by its standing committees to the full council.'[6]

'The Town Clerk of one of our largest cities said to me, knowingly: 'This Act is innocuous. We can drive a carriage and four through it'.'[7]

The indefatigable Charles Arnold-Baker, of the National Association of Parish Councils, lent the full support of his Association [8] but extended the argument as being 'one factor of the more general issue of secrecy in local government', and called for the demise of standing orders, which still existed in some local authorities, governing 'disclosure'.

The crunch came, however, in a further article[9] from the paper's Midlands Correspondent. A random survey, conducted by a number of the paper's staff, of fifty local authorities in the Midlands showed that twenty-seven were not observing the spirit of the Act. It was emphasised that no action had been taken to include 'difficult' authorities or, conversely, to exclude those which were known to enjoy good relations with their local newspapers.

11 of the 50 authorities did not issue committee reports before their council meetings or 'forbade' the press to print any portion of them;
16 allowed factual stories to be written about council proposals but attempted to ban comment on them in any way;
26 of the 50 did not admit the press to *any* committee meetings;
20 admitted the press to one or two committees;
only 4 admitted reporters to more than two committees;
17 neither allowed the press to any committee nor permitted comment on committee reports.

The survey showed no difference in overall response from one major party or the other or, indeed, from independently controlled councils. On non-controversial items the results were a little better, with thirty-seven of the areas professing 'very good' or 'good' relations; seven were only 'fair' and six – even on non-controversial items – were 'difficult'.

The Times staff were not wholly anti-local-authority. In some cases the councils, they said, were merely following custom. The local papers were not always their own best friends – sometimes the authorities were 'aided and abetted' by the local editors. One weekly newspaper editor made his position all too clear: 'I think commenting on minutes is for daily or national papers: they like stirring things up. We do not try it because we have got to live here. If we got the council's back up we should expect to get no facilities from them.'

Perhaps satiated with the previous weeks' letters and articles there was little further correspondence. Apart from Martin Ennals' plaintive cry and a letter from Noel Armstrong (18th January, 1963) praising Norwich Council for its courage and for the effective relations it had with its Press (which, incidentally, mentioned that the misgivings of certain councillors had 'proved groundless') there was little else, except a rather feeble effort by Mr. Denis Howell, M.P.

(later Minister of State, Ministry of Housing and Local Government) to widen the scope of the correspondence. While expressing his support for more open local authority meetings he pointed out the secrecy surrounding the meetings of hospital management committees. His letter evoked no response.

During 1964 complaints still rumbled in various parts of the country and continued into 1965 when the clamour became loud once again. 'The cry has been raised again in places as diverse as Exeter, Barnoldswick, Edinburgh, Berkshire and Bognor.'[10] In fact the situation in Bognor was rather more far-reaching than most. The Clerk of the Council was dismissed at the culmination of a long and involved series of recriminations and counter-recriminations that raised a number of genuine and an even greater number of spurious points of general interest concerning the administration of local government, councillors' personal and pecuniary interests, secrecy and so on.

In view of the general public interest the Minister of Housing and Local Government, Mr. Crossman, appointed Mr. J. Ramsay Willis, Q.C., to hold an inquiry into all the circumstances. The conclusion of this inquiry was, primarily, that the dispute between the Bognor Regis Council and Mr. Paul Smith, the Clerk, had been 'greatly inflated and given the appearance of an issue of national importance due to its largely one-sided presentation in the Press and on television.'[11]

Mr. Smith, the dismissed Clerk, then formed the Local Government Reform Society which had among its main objectives:

1. The admission of the press to all committee meetings with only rigidly controlled exceptions;
2. Committee and council proceedings should be minuted in Hansard form; and,
3. The advertisement of all council and committee meetings in the local press.

Writing in the now defunct magazine *Censorship*[12] Mr. Smith stated: 'If, in a free and democratic society, interest in local affairs is not to deteriorate into apathy, it is vital that the public should be given every opportunity of seeing what their elected representatives are doing in committee, and how they are doing it.'

In the course of his article Mr. Smith quoted examples of council secrecy:

– the case of the Bedfordshire County Hall 'which is having to be rebuilt at a cost to the ratepayers of an additional £250,000. The press reported it in detail and in particular the fact that various Bedfordshire councillors have said that it was advisable 'not to say much about it'.'

– the case of Ploughley R.D.C. where 'the allocation of their council houses is dealt with in secret. Until recently no written report was made by the committee of three councillors who allocated houses.'

– the 'Poole children's committee case.'

At the end of 1965, Dilys Hill of the Department of Politics at the University of Southampton wrote two articles[13] based on a survey of 41 local authorities in the north of England. She was critical of her own methods insofar that any analysis of the problem must depend on concrete examples, 'and so may not be representative of the whole country.'[14]

In view of the comparative smallness of the sample and the danger in applying local findings of this sort to a national context, Dr. Hill was wise not to quote percentages but her articles clearly stated the existing problems:

– local authorities are generally unaccustomed to producing immediate and popularised information;

– local news has to be tied in to personalities and this may lead the authorities to accuse the local press of superficiality;

– the Public Bodies (Admission to Meetings) Act has made little difference to the relationship between the two sides;

– in many towns the press does not want open committees as it cannot cope with attending them;

– the press relies very heavily on council minutes for the bulk of information;

– some authorities discourage officers other than the clerk from communicating with the press, and none of the sample surveyed had a Public Relations Officer;

– the supply of information from local authorities does not always coincide with the newspaper's printing deadlines;

– some authorities placed an embargo on comment before council meetings;

– weekly newspapers cannot compete for topicality with other news media;

– it is easier for the newspaperman to ring the clerk for information than to attend the meeting;

– truly local newspapers are becoming rarer because of amalgamations, etc.;

– the increasing prosperity of a newspaper, or newspaper group, may generate better and wider relations with local government in the ability to devote more time and energy to their affairs;

– 'the relationship between local authorities and the Press, far from being the result of purely political attitudes on the one hand and crusading news-seeking on the other, is largely determined by the size and the resources of both sides.'

Dr. Hill has recently written an interesting book on the participation of residents in the local affairs of their community[15] in which she devotes a chapter to local authorities and the press. Her views have changed little fundamentally over the years but she is concerned that between councils and their public, 'the communication gap has now reached dangerous proportions.'

Questionnaires addressed to local authorities have multiplied tremendously in recent years, and are the bane of many local government officers, and it may be for this reason that the only survey on this subject even approaching comprehensiveness was that conducted by Margaret Harrison and Alan Norton for the Maud Committee on the Management of Local Government.[16] Of the 715 authorities who answered their questionnaire 10 per cent admitted the press to all their main committee meetings, 40 per cent to some main committee meetings and 50 per cent to none. The table on p. 30 is an abbreviated version of that appearing in the Maud Report.

As the survey report explained, 'some committee meetings' may mean anything from 'all except the establishment committee' to 'only the general purposes or the road safety committee.'

Only the Liberal Party, of the three major political

Admission of the Press to Committee Meetings*

Type of Authority	Total Authorities	Number of Authorities admitting the Press to Meetings of					
		Committees			Sub-committees†		
		All	Some	None	All	Some	None
Counties	55	2	32	21	1	5	49
County Boroughs	78	2	46	30	1	17	60
Non-county Boroughs	244	32	99	113	1	13	205
Urban Districts	156	24	56	76	2	4	113
Rural Districts	151	8	51	92	–	–	120
London Boroughs:							
Inner London	12	–	–	12	–	2	10
Outer London	19	1	4	14	–	1	18
TOTAL	715	69	288	358	5	42	575

*Excluding Education Committees, which are required by law to admit the press

†Authorities which do not appoint sub-committees are excluded from these figures.

parties has had the opening up of council committee meetings as part of its official policy for any length of time: a Liberal Party manifesto claims that 'Liberals have been campaigning for a long time for committee meetings to be opened up, and the issue will remain a live one until we control sufficient local authorities ourselves to be able to create a major change of heat in local government thinking throughout the country.'[17]

This is part of the Liberals' campaign for more publicity for council activities generally, wider publicity of planning proposals and regular opportunities for councillors to meet their electors.

In the Labour Party Mr. Crossman and Mr. Greenwood (see chapter 11) made their views well known but it is only more recently that the Labour Party has pronounced officially on the subject. In its discussion document, 'Local Government Reform in England', the National Executive of the Party drew attention to Mr. Greenwood's opinions and recommended that 'the all too frequent exclusion of press and public from vital debates in council committees should be ended.' Three months later the National Executive issued its policy document, 'Principles for Local Government Reform in England', and was even more firm: 'One means of reducing secrecy is to ensure that the Press are admitted to committee meetings whenever possible. The legislation which provides for such admission to full council meetings should, therefore, be extended to cover council committees.'

The National Union of Ratepayers' Associations broadly supports this same line: 'There is only one safeguard ... now that more and more matters are delegated to council committees with power to act. Committees must be thrown open to the public and the Press, subject of course to a committee's right to exclude them only when publicity would be 'contrary to the public interest'.'[18]

1. 27 December, 1962.
2. 31 December, 1962.
3. 1 January, 1963.
4. Martin Ennals, then Secretary of the National Council for Civil Liberties, wrote to *The Times* on 10th January, 1963, in evident hurt that this quotation had been used to defeat arguments put by the N.C.C.L. to Chelmsford Council

when it changed its structure to avoid the terms of the Act.

5. County Councillor Edward W. Havard, 4th January, 1963.

6. John Horley, Chairman, The Conference of Ratepayers Associations of Hendon, 5th January, 1963.

7. Stewart Nicholson, ex-secretary, Institute of Journalists, 8th January, 1963.

8. 7th January, 1963.

9. 8th January, 1963.

10. 'The council and the press', A.J. Beith, Nuffield College, 'New Society', 9th September, 1965.

11. The Report of the Bognor Regis Inquiry, Ministry of Housing & Local Government, 1965, paragraph 310.

12. No. 6, Spring 1966.

13. 'Local authorities and the press.' *Local Government Chronicle,* 4th and 11th December 1965.

14. Ibid, p. 1903.

15. *Participating in Local Affairs.* Penguin Books. 1970.

16. Published as Volume 5 of the Report – *Local Administration in England and Wales.*

17. Extract from Liberal Party manifesto appearing in *Local Council Digest,* Special Political Supplement. 6th April 1968.

18. Extract from N.U.R.A's manifesto appearing in *Local Council Digest,* Special Political Supplement, 6th April 1968.

7 Blyth Spirit

On 17th September, 1969, the Prime Minister, the Rt. Hon. Harold Wilson, O.B.E., M.P., addressed the annual conference of the Association of Municipal Corporations at Scarborough, the first Prime Minister to do so since Gladstone in 1873. His theme was local government reform and in the course of his speech he dwelt on the need for accountability by local authorities to the communities they serve. He recalled Anthony Greenwood's speech to the Labour Party Local Government Conference earlier in the year[1] :

'He pointed out that local authorities are responsible for over one quarter of our national public expenditure and he rightly asserted that the public have a right to know what the council are doing in their name and why they are doing it. As well as removing suspicions about what might be going on behind closed doors at council and even more committee meetings, the admission of the Press is a means of generating a healthy interest in local government. We have the Public Bodies (Admission to Meetings) Act. It needs to be worked in the spirit as well as in the letter, and I endorse the Minister's call to every councillor to search his conscience on the way his council operates that Act.'

Among his audience was Alderman Fred Smith, the leader of Blyth Borough Council, and Councillor William Woolfrey, chairman of the Council's establishments committee. Whether they squirmed in their seats only they or perhaps the Town Clerk, Edward Carter, who accompanied them, can tell. Certainly they *should* have felt uncomfortable although from all events this seems unlikely. Indeed, within a few days the two members were present at a council committee meeting which recommended that a copy of the Prime Minister's speech should be circulated to every council member. Which is all very strange because at that time Alderman Smith and his colleagues were involved in a mighty tussle to exclude the local Press from their committee meetings – in defiance of Mr. Wilson's advice.

The question of admitting the Press to committees had come up at various times over the years but this latest bid began in July, 1969, when the lone Liberal councillor, Raymond McClure, in pursuit of official Liberal Party policy proposed in the *Blyth News/Advertiser* that the Press and public should be admitted to Blyth Council's committee meetings.[2] Quoting from a number of the speeches and statements to be found elsewhere in this book, he presented his case in which he specified a particular instance when committee secrecy had, for a time, placed Blyth children at risk from an acid polluted stream. In spite of this Alderman Smith thought Councillor McClure's suggestion was 'plainly ridiculous'.

'People', declared the Alderman, 'are not generally interested in coming to meetings.'

Then, oddly, he criticised Councillor McClure for suggesting that the establishments committee should be exempted from Press admission. If the Press were coming in he said they would be in to the establishments committee but as they weren't they wouldn't be ... !

Alderman Smith's objections were clearly historically based:

'I remember sitting in the Council benches some years ago at a time when it was impossible to count the number of times a reporter's pencil was put down when a Labour member stood up to speak. They are still hostile and we still wouldn't get a fair share of publicity.'

The motion was rejected by 28 votes to 5, four independent councillors voting with Councillor McClure, the majority being composed entirely of Labour members. And there, for the time being – doubtless the summer council recess had much to do with it – the matter rested. The publication of the Labour Party's discussion document on local government reform[3] on 7th September, 1969 inspired the chairman of Blyth Liberals to write to the *News*

Advertiser asking whether in view of the document's suggestion[4] to open up more committees a change of heart might be expected from Blyth Council.[5]

Blyth is a growing industrial centre and sea port. Situated right up in the north east corner of England with the Scottish border only some 30 miles away it has been described in at least one guide book[6] as a grimy place with nothing to detain the visitor. It has a population of about 35,500 (23,000 electors), a rateable value of just under £1 million, about 5,000 council houses and a recently opened 65-acre light industrial trading estate. The town's affairs are covered not only by the *Blyth News/Advertiser* but also by *The Journal, Newcastle* which on 16th October, 1969, let loose a major attack on the Council for what it described in a stormy editorial as 'a deplorable state of affairs.' In no less than five coordinated articles in that day's paper *The Journal* detailed the issues at stake, the Whitehall view, the local councillors' views and its own strong views on the situation.

In an effort to find out the opinions of individual Council members on admission of the Press to committees as many of them as possible were contacted by reporters. *The Journal's* own article sums up the results best:

'Here is the reaction of the members to the questions: The Mayor, Alderman Mrs. L.M. Sumners (Lab.): 'No comment.' Alderman E. Breadin (Lab.): 'No comment.' Alderman T.G. Elder (Lab.): 'No comment.' Alderman A. Rutherford (Lab.): 'No comment.' Alderman J. Tweddle (Lab.): 'No comment.' Councillor R.B. Anderson (Lab.): 'No comment.' Councillor N. Batchelor (Lab.): 'No comment.' Councillor W. Blades (Lab.): 'No comment.' Councillor Mrs. P.M. Bradin (Lab.): 'No comment.' ...'

and so the dreary list dragged on through 25 Labour members. Two of the Labour side were persuaded to say a little more. Alderman Mrs. M. Purves thought that open committees would stifle free debate while the ubiquitous Alderman Smith restated his objections:

'I have never felt that we, the Labour members, have had a fair deal. I am not prepared to think the Press is impartial in its reporting.'

Of the other councillors interviewed at least four of the Independents and, of course, Liberal Councillor McClure, favoured open committees. One Independent was obviously opposed and the others gave ambiguous answers.

Not surprisingly the accompanying editorial was tart:

'We would respect the Labour leadership more if it allowed councillors to speak their minds on this immensely important issue.'

The Journal's feature had been published on the day of a Council meeting at which Councillor McClure again raised the question of admission to committees. At a sparsely attended Council meeting he lost again, 17-6. No less than 14 Labour members were absent from the meeting and the impression was that having failed to agree on a compromise course of action at the pre-council group meeting the dissenting Labour councillors decided, or were told, to stay away.

What most shocked Councillor McClure and *The Journal* was the procedural move engineered by newly elevated Alderman John Hudspith who succeeded in cutting off all further discussion on the motion on the grounds that: 'We have gone right through all this before.'[7]

The entire Council meeting lasted 18 minutes.

But now reaction came from the local M.P., Mr. Edward Milne,[8] who made it known that he was putting down a question for the Minister of Housing and Local Government to answer. Using the Parliamentary precedent of fully reported debates Mr. Milne said:

'We have always held the view that people who enter public life and undertake public activities should conduct their activities in public.'[9]

One of the Independent councillors stifled at the Council meeting took what *The Journal* called 'the unprecedented step[10] of publishing the speech he would have made had he been allowed. Surprisingly, the statement was wary of more Press admission in case party whipping should extend to committees also. The action at the Council meeting also provoked a Mr. W.R. Sullivan[11] 'to write to both *The Journal* and the *News/Advertiser* to protest about the 'complete negation of democratic government.'

Supporting Mr. Milne and the official Labour Party view, the Blyth Labour Party secretary-agent Peter Mortakis, a former councillor, stepped into the fray with a statement[12] in which he doubted Councillor McClure's sincerity but, nevertheless wondered why Blyth Council could not achieve a reasonable relationship with the Press as, for example, nearby Bedlington Council had achieved. 'We have,' he said, 'to acknowledge the role that newspapers have to play in political and local government affairs.'

Mr. Milne weighed in again. Speaking to the Blyth Labour Women's Federation he attacked the indecision and ineffectiveness of the Council leadership but pointed out that the Press had responsibilities also.

He was quickly joined by the Conservative Parliamentary candidate, Mr. A.J. Blackburn, who was not going to let the Labour split go unremarked:

'Blyth has been their 'pocket borough' for as long as they can remember. For so long that they have forgotten about the people who elected them.'[13]

The next twist in the plot came when the successful Labour candidate for the Croft Ward declared roundly that he supported: 'The Prime Minister, Mr. Anthony Greenwood and the Labour Party headquarters'[14]
and favoured opening up committees. His electoral success encouraged both *The Journal* and the *News/Advertiser* to optimistic editorials. Their optimism was short-lived.

At the November council meeting, (described as '... one of the longest council meetings in recent years,' it lasted just over half an hour in a display of incredibly thick-skin, two committee chairmen asked the local Press to give publicity to matters discussed in private committees. *The Journal*'s next editorial was a trifle righteous:

'Because *The Journal* believes that the electors of Blyth have a right to know what the people they voted for are doing in their name, we have given the publicity requested.'[15]

In the meantime behind-the-scenes activities continued. The Minister had answered Mr. Milne's question in the Commons, stating:

'Local authorities are already well aware of the great importance the Minister attaches to their keeping the Press and public informed of their activities.[16]

Mr. Mortakis had written to Transport House appealing for help or advice. The Liberals asked the Prime Minister to intervene but he explained that although his views were well known there was no way that he could insist on his views being adopted.[17]

Perhaps in an effort to take some of the heat off at its December meeting the Council decided to hold 'any questions' sessions at future meetings.[18] The idea is said to have emanated from a suggestion made by Edward Milne for 'open council meetings' more than a year before. Liberal Councillor McClure was convinced it was just a sop to prevent the opening of committees and noted that questions could not be asked until after the decisions had been taken. He voted against but some of the Independent councillors supported the move as a step in the right direction.

Because of the controversy and to counter charges of partiality *The Journal* opened its columns to Alderman Smith who put his case[19] in 1,200 words – from which the following extracts are taken:–

'Evidence suggests that there is very little interest in Council affairs and because of this people are entitled to ensure that, in a very large measure, the public are satisfied with their town's management ...'

'It has been suggested that the Council may have something to hide. How anything can be hidden is difficult to understand ...'

'Officials have their appointments and reputations to preserve, very few step out of line, and Blyth can boast of a reliable and efficient team of officers ...'

'It is unjust, incorrect and untrue to suggest that either there is anything to hide or that the public are demanding to know more than that with which they are at present provided ...'

'No one has ever refused to supply information sought of a councillor by any member of the public ...'

'The accommodation is just not there to meet any kind of exceptional demand, and to argue that provision should be made to accommodate a few is to acknowledge that the interest in attending meetings is negligible.'

Writing of the 'no comment' story,[20] Alderman Smith pleaded:

'Don't try to read into a situation anything more than exists. It was merely an absence of inclination that prevented people from replying, and a reluctance on the part of some people to see their name in print.'

He denied that the membership of the housing committee had been artificially held down so that it was one or two below the statutory limit[21] for the admission of the Press to its meetings.

In an attempt at humour: 'We appreciate the vested interest the Press has in the situation and make allowances.'

In a Freudian slip: 'The leaders do not make decisions.'

In a crack at Mr. Milne: 'When there is a difference of opinion between the Prime Minister and someone else, it must exist in the cases of either abstention or voting against Mr. Wilson,[22] then is it to be argued that Mr. Wilson should resign or should be removed?'

The Journal staff reporter attempted a reply to those points that could be replied to. In particular he picked up Alderman Smith's assertion that information was never withheld –

'In each case, inquiries were made at the Council's offices and in each case I was informed that the information I sought was not available.'[23]

In a last desperate throw following the publication of the Labour Party's principles for local government reform [24] Peter Mortakis said:

'I hope that now this document has been released, *all* authorities controlled by Labour Party members will take note and act upon the recommendations that have been made by the national executive committee.[25]

The Council remained unmoved.

In a final ironic twist at the first Council 'any questions' session the two people in the public gallery walked out during the Mayor's introductory speech.[26]

1. Harrogate, 15th February, 1969.
2. *Blyth News/Advertiser.* 17th July, 1969.
3. *Local Government Reform in England.* Labour Party. See p.
4. *Ibid.*, page 21.
5. *News/Advertiser.* 11th September, 1969.
6. *Guide to the Northumberland Coast.* Ward Lock and Co. Ltd.
7. *Journal.* 17th October, 1969.
8. 23,000+ majority; first elected 1960, in a by-election; ex USDAW organiser; a Scotsman.
9. *Journal,* 17th October, 1969.

10. *Journal,* 18th October, 1969.
11. Member of the Council for the years 1953–1967; Chief Warden of the Borough, 1942.
12. *Journal,* 21st October, 1969.
13. *Journal,* 27th October, 1969.
14. *Journal,* 4th November, 1969.
15. *Journal,* 14th November, 1969.
16. H.C. Written Ans., 18th November, 1969. Vol.791, col. 254.
17. *Journal,* 22nd November, 1969.
18. *News/Advertiser,* 18th December, 1969.
19. *Journal,* 17th December, 1969.
20. See p. 35.
21. Section 2, Public Bodies (Admission to Meetings) Act, 1960.
22. Mr. Milne has been known to do both.
23. *Journal,* 23rd December, 1969.
24. *Principles for Local Government Reform in England.* Labour Party. 28th December, 1969.
25. *Journal,* 30th December, 1969.
26. *Journal,* 9th January, 1970.

8 Local Authorities and the Press Council — 1

Wherever and whenever local authority-Press relations are discussed there will be found a number of local authority members who detail the irritations that they have suffered at the hands of the local Press and particulars of these irritations are frequently advanced. In this, of course, councillors are no different from M.P.s, civil servants, bishops or other public figures who have suffered at the hand of a critical Press. It is impossible to categorise scientifically these irritations and in an extended conversation it is frequently found that a particular irritation may well be a matter of hurt pride rather than a serious complaint of general, rather than personal, interest. Candidates for public office should, perhaps, be advised that a broad back is, or should be, part of their normal equipment.

But there *are* more serious complaints. The Maud Committee on the Management of Local Government said[1] that most of these criticisms refer to sensationalism, inaccuracies or bad coverage but different chairmen in the same authority made remarks that 'tended to cancel each other out'.

'It is obvious,' stated the Committee in a grand under-statement, 'that subjective standards vary a great deal on what may be reasonably expected of the Press in terms of comment and general coverage'.[2]

An attempt to achieve some sort of standard can be obtained by examining the complaints that have been made to the Press Council and which have been adjudicated upon.

The Press Council was established as the General Council of the Press in 1953, and reconstituted in 1963 with a lay chairman and 25 members. It has a number of aims, among them to preserve the established freedom of the British Press and to deal with complaints about the conduct of the Press or the conduct of persons or organisations towards the Press. Other aims include the promotion of training for journalists; technical research; the study of trends towards monopoly, etc. The Council publishes an annual report which, in abbreviated form, details the cases upon which it has adjudicated during the preceding year and a study of the published adjudications in the years since 1960, when the Public Bodies (Admission to Meetings) Act 1960 was enacted, is revealing.

Ignoring a very few complaints by individual councillors – who were generally complaining as private citizens about matters not specifically connected with local government – there had been, until July, 1968, about 50 complaints by local authorities, or local authority officers acting in their official capacities, against the Press on which adjudications have been published, an average of just over 5 complaints a year. Of these complaints 45 per cent were directed at national or provincial dailies and Sundays, the remainder being against local newspapers.[3]

Of the complaints against national newspapers 57 per cent were upheld by the Press Council as being justified while 44 per cent of the complaints against local newspapers were similarly upheld. In fact, 12 complaints against local newspapers in nine years have been held to be wholly justified – there have been one or two partial upholdings of complaints where it was felt that the blame for a particular incident might be apportioned between both parties. Even allowing for the fact that many complaints do not reach the stage of an official adjudication, being settled or withdrawn following advice or information tendered by one of the staff of the Press Council, these figures do indicate a very much less serious situation than casual conversation with councillors would lead one to believe.

An examination of some of the complaints upheld is, however, of interest:

Complaint and Correction[4]

The Walsall Town Council and the Willenhall Urban

District Council protested to the Press Council about an article in the *Sunday Pictorial* which alleged that these local authorities, among others, had sold the addresses of bad paying tenants to a private credit traders' organisation. The *Sunday Pictorial* admitted to the Press Council that it had been misinformed and had published a correction a fortnight after the appearance of the original article.

The two Councils decided to proceed with their complaint as they felt that more care should be taken by newspapers to ascertain the accuracy of information before publication and that the same prominence should be given to the correction as to the original article.

The Press Council, while noting that the *Sunday Pictorial* published a correction in the first available issue after the complaint was made to it, considered that not enough care was taken to obtain accurate information from the local authorities concerned before the article was published.

Photographed in School[5]

The Kent Education Authority took exception to an article and picture in the *Daily Mail* of 31st March, 1961. It was claimed that on the day of an examination when regulations excluded from the test rooms all persons other than pupils and supervisors, the headmistress refused permission for the taking of Press photographs. After the examination, representatives of the *Daily Mail* took a boy pupil into the school and photographed him there. It was submitted that this constituted 'unwarranted intrusion.' The Committee also urged that inaccuracies in the article might affect public confidence in teaching procedure.

The Press Council considered that the *Daily Mail* representatives were guilty of intrusion in interviewing a pupil inside the school on the day of an examination and also of taking photographs in a classroom despite the refusal of the headmistress to permit the taking of pictures. The Council added: 'The newspaper described incorrectly the nature of the examination and this mistake, in its view, could have been avoided if full inquiries had been made.'

The Need For Frankness[6]

Ilford Borough Council complained about the way in which the *Ilford Recorder* had obtained an exclusive picture of Mr. Frederick Gibberd's model of the architectural design for Ilford's new town centre. The Borough Council argued that it was unethical and seriously damaging to good relationship between the Council and the Press.

Mr. F.B. Nicholls, the Town Clerk, informed the Press Council that it had been thought desirable that preparation of a statement and photograph for the Press should be left to the designing architect and the *Ilford Recorder* was told that this official Press release would be issued as soon as possible. Some days later a woman purporting to speak on behalf of an unspecified firm of architects, obtained by telephone from Mr. Gibberd's office the identity and location of his model makers. On the same day a man saying he represented the *Ilford Recorder* telephoned the architect's secretary for permission to photograph the model. This was refused. On the following day two young men called at the model factory and twice assured the manager that they had Mr. Gibberd's permission to photograph the model. Two days later the newspaper published an exclusive picture, after having been told by Mr. Gibberd's secretary, in his absence, that sanction to print could not be given.

The Town Clerk complained that the identity of the model makers had been obtained by misrepresentation; that the factory manager had been misled; that the persons concerned had all been employed by the *Ilford Recorder,* and that the photograph had been published in defiance of unequivocal refusal, by the owner or owners, of permission to reproduce it.

Mr. L.J. Sims, editor of the *Ilford Recorder,* declared that publication of the picture was the result of journalistic resource in the face of lack of understanding by officialdom of the needs of the Press in a matter of vital public interest. Although the Town Clerk was authorised to report on the civic centre scheme, the weekly Press conference was cancelled and his paper was asked to 'hold its horses' until the official handout was ready, probably in the following week. He did not give any undertaking to observe this arrangement. He insisted that no effort was ever considered or made to deceive the factory manager.

The Press Council's adjudication was: 'In a matter of such vital interest and importance to a town it is the local newspaper's function to publish all available information and photographs as soon as possible. But a duty is also laid on the newspaper to pursue its inquiries with complete frankness and the Press Council is satisfied that the *Ilford Recorder* did not do so. To that extent it was at fault.'

Unsubstantiated[7]

Is there a spy in the Council Office? asked the *Essex Weekly News* in the heading to a news story that told of a woman who inquired at Brentwood Urban District Council Offices about building permission in relation to a plot of land she had been offered 'for a song'. Within an hour, the story said, she returned to the owner of the plot only to find that local building contractors had bought the land for a higher figure than she had been asked. She stated that nobody else could possibly have known about the proposed deal and was reported to have said '... it all points to there being someone at the Council tipping off the big building contractors ... I feel sure there is something shady going on and it ought to be investigated.'

The story described the woman as wishing to remain anonymous and the newspaper observed: 'We cannot vouch for her story. We give it because we feel it should be investigated.'

Mr. E.E.W. Hornbrook, of 278 Priests Lane, Shenfield, complained to the Press Council that the publication was despicable because it sought to cast doubts upon the integrity of Council employees without a whiff of evidence.

Both Mr. Clement Booth, Clerk to Brentwood U.D.C. and Mr. J.H.T. Hack, president of Brentwood (Local Govt.) Branch of NALGO regarded the innuendo as damaging, distressing and unjustified.

Mr. E.L. Waring, editor, *Essex Weekly News* stated he felt the matter should be aired because the person who complained was so emphatic that she and the owner of the land were the only people who knew she wished to buy. He still felt he did right in throwing the matter open for inquiry and reply.

The Press Council found that the newspaper should not have published the story which was based on the unsubstantiated assumption of an aggrieved person. There was no evidence to support it, nor was the newspaper able to obtain any.

What Is A Reasonable Time?[8]

What is a reasonable time for a newspaper to make a night telephone call to a responsible council official for information?

Mr. E.R. Davies, Clerk to the Berkshire County Council, complained to the Press Council that a *Daily Express* staff reporter telephoned him about 12-30 to 1 a.m. when he was in bed and asleep to confirm a news report about the action of his Council in requiring its employees to hand over trading stamps received on the purchase of petrol for Council-owned-motor-cars.

Mr. Davies said that while it was his duty, as a public official, to assist the Press, it was an intolerable intrusion into his privacy to be awakened in the middle of the night on a matter that was neither urgent nor important.

Mr. Robert Edwards, then Editor, *Daily Express,* said that the telephone call was made shortly before midnight. It did not seem to him to be an abuse to telephone a responsible official on a matter concerning his Council at such a time. Checking to avoid inaccurate reporting had to be done sometimes at night, but considerable care was taken to ensure that this was not done wantonly.

Mr. Edwards submitted evidence that the reporter who made the call finished telephoning his report to the *Daily Express* office at 12-26 a.m. after having made three other telephone calls and writing the news-story.

The adjudication was: 'The Press Council reaffirms the need for exercise by newspapers of the greatest care in making telephone calls for information late at night. In this instance the Council does not feel that the matter was sufficiently important to justify the inquiry made by the *Daily Express.*'

Phrase Not Justified[9]

The phrase 'escape disaster by the skin of one's teeth' set the Press Council a problem. It arose out of a complaint from Canvey Island U.D.C. that a report in the *Daily Express* relating to damage to the island sea defences was inaccurate, irresponsible and calculated to cause undue anxiety in the minds of residents.

The newspaper account said 'Last night the Island escaped by the skin of its teeth as huge waves battered the new defences. The stonework cracked; parts of it crumbled and but for the massive steel piling the sea would have swept through'. It was termed a 'near disaster'.

Mr. L. Lock-Dingley, Clerk to the Council, stated that at no time was there any question of the Island escaping flooding 'by the skin of its teeth'. The outer stone facing work of the sea wall was severely damaged by wind and wave action but the stone facing was there for the purpose of protecting the earth embankment sea wall behind it. There was no danger of the sea wall being pierced.

Mr. E.L. Snell, Engineer to the Essex River Board, told the Press Council that he inspected the sea defences during the day of the storm and was satisfied that at no time was there any danger of the wall being breached or of flooding occurring.

Mr. Robert Edwards, editor, *Daily Express,* stated it was agreed by everyone that the damage to the wall at Canvey Island was very extensive. The wind dropped at a crucial time. Like the local Ratepayers' Association, he wondered what would have happened if it had not.

The adjudication was: 'The Press Council considers that the *Daily Express* was not justified in using the phrase 'near disaster' in reporting the high tides and gale which visited Canvey Island in January.'

Councillors As Reporters[10]

Daventry Borough Council, through its Town Clerk, Mr. Arthur E. Moore, complained that a *Daventry and District Weekly Express* report of a finance and general purposes committee meeting, admittedly 'picked up' from two Council members, was inaccurate. The meeting was open to the Press but no representatives attended.

The report, dealing with a discussion about the principle to be adopted in dealing with owner-shopkeepers who would be displaced under a development scheme, contained a statement that Alderman G. Williams had remarked, 'There will not be a square inch of freehold interest left in Daventry.' Alderman Williams denied having made that statement.

The report also stated that Councillor E.H. Beech supported Alderman Williams in all he had said. That was not true, said the Town Clerk, regarding the remark attributed to Alderman Williams but which was not made. A further reference in the report stated that Alderman W.G.S. Edwards did not take part in the discussion. That was untrue, said the Town Clerk. He did contribute to the debate..

In a later issue the *Weekly Express* published a front-page story which recorded that the report was obtained from two members of the Council who attended the committee meeting. Then followed the full text of the Town Clerk's letter of complaint to the Press Council on behalf of the Mayor and members of the Borough Council.

In a feature article in the same issue, the newspaper said'... the *Weekly Express* accepts that Council members are perhaps not quite as accurate in their reporting as trained journalists.'

Mr. W.R. Green, editor, *Weekly Express,* told the Press Council that he saw Council members coming away from the finance committee meeting. Councillor Moser told him that Alderman G. Williams had said that all freeholds in the town were threatened. Next day he saw Councillor Moser again and made some shorthand notes of what he told him.

Mr. Green gave an account of a later meeting of the finance committee at which, according to his record, Councillor Moser said there was no doubt in his mind that at the earlier meeting Alderman Williams had said three times there would not be a square inch of freehold in the town centre and had retracted it three times.

Councillor R.B. Moser told the Press Council that Alderman Williams did utter the words 'There will not be a square inch of freehold left in Daventry' at least once during the meeting.

Councillor John Cockerill said he fully agreed with what Mr. Green had published.

The Press Council's adjudication stated:

(a) In this case it was wrong for the *Daventry and District Weekly Express* to report in the form of direct quotation words said to have been used by a Council member at a meeting open to the Press which no newspaper representative attended. In this respect the complaint is upheld.

(b) The publication of the letter of correction from the Town Clerk dated 3rd August 1965, was, in the circumstances, sufficient to balance the report and in this respect the complaint is rejected.

Words Transposed[11]

The *Scottish Daily Express* printed a report headed 'Motorists rage, but parking is so easy here', in which the car-parking arrangements for Glasgow councillors were compared with those afforded the public.

The article contained the passage: 'Highways committee convener, Councillor Jeremiah O'Sullivan, who shocked motorists on Wednesday with the announcement that the Corporation intends to 'price' all-day parkers out of the city, used a Council car yesterday morning to take him to the Central Police Court. And he insisted that he was not anti-motorist simply because he is not a driver'.

Councillor O'Sullivan denied that he made the quoted statement. He said 'I drive a car and indeed, paid my insurance renewal for it last January.' He asked the newspaper to retract the error.

Mr. John E. Campbell, managing editor, *Scottish Daily Express,* replied that having a driving licence did not make Councillor O'Sullivan a motorist, but if he said that he owned a car and drove regularly the newspaper would make the situation clear to its readers.

Mr. Clive Sandground, deputy editor of the newspaper, told the Council that the exact words of Councillor O'Sullivan were: 'It is not true to say that I am against drivers because I am not a motorist.' In transcribing that remark into direct speech the words 'motorist' and 'driver' were transposed but there was no significant difference in the two words considered in the context of the article.

The adjudication of the Press Council was: 'The *Scottish Daily Express* made an incorrect statement about Councillor O'Sullivan and should have corrected it when requested. The complaint is upheld.'

Local Authority Upheld[12]

Llantrisant and Llantwit Fardre R.D.C. accused the *Western Mail* and the *South Wales Echo* of inaccuraries in a report relating to a proposed charge for services performed by the Council and further complained that the newspapers failed to publish an apology or explanation.

Both reports concerned a deputation from Pontypridd and Rhondda hospital management committee to the finance committee of Llantrisant and Llantwit Fardre R.D.C. asking for reconsideration of a proposed charge for removing ash from the new boiler system at the East Glamorgan Hospital, Church Village.

The opening paragraph of the *Western Mail* report read: 'A South Wales local council was attacked last night for insisting on payment for collecting ash from a hospital's boiler system. The expense, put at about £600 a year, would mean patients would have to go without some services, it was said.'

The *South Wales Echo* report began: 'Llantrisant and Llantwit Fardre R.D.C. was last night accused of 'depriving' patients by charging up to £50 a week for the collection of ash from the boiler at East Glamorgan Hospital in addition to the weekly rates of nearly £50.'

Mr. Geoffrey Hockin, Clerk to the R.D.C. sent one letter to the 'Editor, *Western Mail* and *South Wales Echo* challenging the figures and complaining of 'careless and misleading journalism'. He told the Press Council that a report by his Council's Treasurer, Mr. R.J. Brown, that set out with perfect clarity the financial implications of the ash collection was available to the Press before the meeting. He objected to the newspaper's statement that the Council had been 'attacked' and said that the figures quoted had been 'wildly exaggerated'.

Mr. Russell Lyne, a *Western Mail* reporter, asserted that Mr. Hockin had said that a correction in the *Western Mail* was not necessary and with Mr. Brown had confirmed that the newspaper's figure was correct.

Mr. Ross Davies, *Western Mail* and *South Wales Echo* staff reporter at Pontypridd, who attended the meeting and wrote both reports, stated that he did not recall the provision of any printed statement about the finances of ash removal. The figure 'up to £50 a week' was a balance between two figures used at the meeting.

Mr. John Giddings, editor, *Western Mail,* answering the complaints, said that the figure given in his newspaper was factual. It had since been confirmed as that given during the discussion. The word 'attacked' was used in the introduction to the report as a synonym for 'criticised'. Mr. John H. Wiggins, editor, *South Wales Echo,* told the Press Council that he would have been prepared to clear up any misunderstanding if he had been aware of the complaint at the time.

Mr. R.J. Brown gave evidence that he confirmed to the *Western Mail* that £600 a year was the cost of the removal. The amount charged to the hospital management committee was only half that.

Mr. Ross Davies, in oral evidence, said he made it clear that the total expense of ash removal was £600 a year and that the Hospital would be asked to defray about half that cost. His introduction in the *Western Mail* had been completely rewritten and he had complained about it.

The Press Council's adjudication was: 'The reports in both the *Western Mail* and the *South Wales Echo* gave misleading and inaccurate accounts of what had taken place at the meeting and of the atmosphere there. The complaint is upheld.'

An examination of these cases, which have been selected in order to give as wide a view as possible of the sort of complaint made, but have not otherwise been specially chosen, shows quite clearly that there is no pattern of a particular type of complaint common from all local authorities. This would seem to reinforce the Maud Committee's statement that subjective standards must vary a great deal.

1. Volume 5. Local Government Administration in England and Wales, Chapter 17, para. 34.
2. *Ibid.,* para. 34.
3. At that date there were 30 morning newspapers, 77 evening, 14 Sunday and 1,160 weekly and bi-weekly newspapers (15th Annual Report of the Press Council, p. 136).
4. 7th annual report of the Press Council, p. 33.
5. 8th annual report of the Press Council, p. 23.
6. 9th annual report of the Press Council, pp. 43–44.
7. 10th annual report of the Press Council, pp. 40–41.
8. 11th annual report of the Press Council, p. 35.
9. 12th annual report of the Press Council, pp. 31–32.
10. 13th annual report of the Press Council, pp. 49–50.
11. 14th annual report of the Press Council, pp. 90–91.
12. 15th annual report of the Press Council, pp. 11–12.

9 Local Authorities and the Press Council – 2

Not all complaints to the Press Council with which we are concerned emanate from local authorities about the Press. Two most important complaints dealt with in 1966-67 and 1967-68 were *about* local authorities.

The first complaint came from the director of a news and photo agency in Bournemouth who complained that the formalities of the Public Bodies (Admission to Meetings) Act, 1960 had not been complied with. The Press Council upheld his complaint and the full adjudication is reproduced at the end of this Chapter.

The second case arose from the complaint of the Wiltshire and Gloucestershire District of the Institute of Journalists and the Gloucestershire branch of the National Union of Journalists about their exclusion from a meeting of the Cheltenham Borough Council for inadequate reasons and about derogatory remarks made by the Town Clerk. Again the complaint was upheld and the adjudication will be found in full at the end of this Chapter.

Strictures on local authorities may also be found in the course of adjudications on complaints from the local authority where the Press Council has felt that the council has not done all that it might to ensure co-operation. For instance, in 1959-60 the Press Council reported on a complaint from Earby U.D.C.:

Right Of Publication[1]

The Clerk to the Earby Urban District Council, Lancashire, complained about the publication of an article in the *Barnoldswick and Earby Times* which dealt with the proposed conversion of a local cinema into a public hall and swimming bath.

When this came before the Council's general purposes committee, the minute was marked 'Not for Publication' but in spite of this the newspaper published an article relating to the matter. Publication did not take place, however, until after the matter had been considered in open Council at a later date. Nevertheless, the Council decided to exclude representatives of the newspaper from future meetings and to cease to supply agenda, reports and minutes to the editor.

The Press Council declared that the editor had a full right to publish the news once it had come before the full meeting of the Council and regretted the action the Council took against the *Barnoldswick and Earby Times.*

And again, criticising a council's over-sensitivity:

A Statement Refuted[2]

Should a newspaper, as a point of principle, withhold publication of a responsible organisation's statement on public affairs because some of its content is contested by another public body which wishes to consider its terms of refutation?

This issue came before the Press Council when Mr. N.F.E. Browning, Clerk to Winsford (Cheshire) Urban District Council, complained of a report published in the *Manchester Evening News* under the heading 'Overspill homes 'standing empty'.' This stated that Winsford Ratepayers' Association claimed that Manchester's overspill scheme at Winsford had failed and that Winsford Council was having to speed up demolition schemes to fill empty houses.

Mr. Browning wrote to the editor of the *Manchester Evening News,* saying that one of the newspaper's reporters, by telephone, had invited his comments on the statements of the Ratepayers' Association. He had replied that parts of the statement were patently inaccurate, but he was not prepared to comment extemporaneously. The reporter, Mr. Browning stated, said that the matter had to be published that day. Mr. Browning said he gave the reporter figures of building and employment.

Mr. T.E. Henry, editor-in-chief, *Manchester Evening News,* replying to this letter, said that the Ratepayers' Association's views had been reported reasonably and accurately, and Mr. Browning had been told what the Association had said and had rejected an opportunity to reply.

To the Press Council, Mr. Browning complained of inaccuracy. The issue was one of deliberate publication of falsehood in preference to truth. He raised as a subsidiary issue the question whether a newspaper has the right to coerce anyone into giving an extemporaneous comment over the telephone under the implied threat that if he does not do so information in the hands of the paper will be published irrespective of its truth or falsity.

Replying to the complaint, Mr. Henry said that when Mr. Browning was spoken to he expressed his dislike of the Ratepayers' Association and persistently refused to comment. At no time since publication of the report had Mr. Browning asked the newspaper to publish any rebuttal, although this would have been done at his request.

The adjudication was: 'The Press Council considers that the *Manchester Evening News* afforded Winsford Urban District Council a reasonable opportunity of stating for publication the gist of the Council's point of view in reply to the statement by the local Ratepayers' Association. Consequently, the Council rejects the complaint.'

Below are appended the Press Council's two adjudications on the complaints about exclusion of the Press from local authority meetings mentioned above.

A. Press Improperly Excluded From Council Meeting

The way in which Press representatives were excluded from a meeting of Bournemouth County Borough Council, called to discuss a confidential report on administrative efficiency in the municipal offices, was criticised by the Press Council.

Mr. Graham Mole, director, Forest News and Photo Agency, Bournemouth Ltd., Yelverton Road, Bournemouth, complained that when he went to report a meeting of 'the whole Council in committee' he was asked by the Mayor,

Alderman Philip Whitelegg, to leave. A councillor suggested that there should be a resolution, but the Town Clerk, Mr. A. Lindsay Clegg, replied 'No' and the Mayor said that the meeting had been 'called in committee'. Mr. Mole left.

When he returned to the meeting, then being held in open session, there was no debate about the preceding deliberations and he was subsequently left to interview the chairman of the management techniques committee, who handed him a copy of the speech he had made to the Council in committee. This revealed, said Mr. Mole, that management consultants hired by the Council had said that by increasing efficiency £109,000 a year of the ratepayers' money could be saved.

Mr. Mole contended that he had been improperly asked to leave the meeting and that in doing so the Council acted against the spirit of the Minister of Housing and Local Government's advice to councils with regard to the Public Bodies (Admission to Meetings) Act, 1960.

Mr. Lindsay Clegg informed the Press Council that the Council had engaged managerial consultants to provide two reports, the first on departmental organisation and administration and the second on the overall municipal and committee structure. The management techniques committee decided to circulate the first report to members on a private and confidential basis. This was because it was incomplete without the second report which had not, at that time, been received; possibly critical of individuals or committees who had not seen it before and because some Council members were known to be in disagreement with some of the proposals.

It was decided to submit the first report to the Council in private and to follow consideration with a public meeting. Notice of the latter meeting was given in the ordinary way. At the beginning of the private meeting a motion was properly moved and seconded that the Press should be allowed to remain, but having regard to the confidential aspect of the matter at that stage, the motion was defeated on a vote.

The Town Clerk also said that, within days, certain national newspapers reacted violently to the incident and the Bournemouth Council, who had acted quite properly and in good faith, was subjected to extreme and 'snowballing' criticism which suggested that his Council was engaged in some sinister impropriety to the detriment of the public when, throughout, its desire had been to handle the matter in a businesslike and intelligible way in the ratepayers' best interests. His Council was not hostile to the Press and its arrangements for Press relations were better than in many places. No harm to the public or obstruction of the Press had ever been intended by the Council.

In answer to Press Council inquiries, the Town Clerk said that the notice of the meeting in private had been in the form of a private and confidential letter to members. He agreed that when the meeting of the Council in committee was about to begin the reporters had been asked by the Mayor to withdraw. They had left and then it was moved that the Press be admitted. It would have been better if the resolution had followed the words of the appropriate section of the Act, but it was not unlawful, in the circumstances, to exclude the Press. The reason for exclusion was printed and the Press and the public were fully aware of the intention to consider the report, in the first instance, in committee.

Commenting on the incident, the Press Council stated that it had reason to believe that relations between the local authority and the Press in Bournemouth were good, but it appears that, in the particular instance, the Press were improperly excluded from the meeting. The Council added that the Town Clerk's statement that it was a technicality could not be accepted because it was of vital importance, firstly, that in such circumstances the resolution to exclude the Press should be debated in public and, secondly, that the reasons for the Council resolving itself into committee should be stated in the resolution.

From 14th annual report of the Press Council, pp.30-32.

B. Improper Exclusion of the Press

Commenting for the second time within a year on the exclusion of representatives of the Press from local authority meetings, the Press Council issued a statement in April, 1968, calling attention to the necessity for strict compliance with the law affecting the admission of the Press to such meetings.

The Council considered representations made by the Wilts and Gloucestershire District of the Institute of Journalists and the Gloucestershire branch of the National Union of Journalists following a meeting of Cheltenham Borough Council to discuss a £528,000 swimming pool scheme and other development projects.

The journalists complained that when the Town Clerk, Mr. A.A. Crabtree, was invited at the meeting to advise the Council on whether or not it should exclude the Press and public, he advised the Council to discuss a report on the projects in private, adding 'There is no question of dealing with money behind locked doors because you are not going to spend anything at all tonight.' The journalists said that he went on to describe a report in a local evening newspaper as 'very inaccurate and misleading', adding, 'if this is the standard of reporting of meetings, the Press ought to be excluded from such meetings.' The journalists contended that the criticism was without foundation and was an unwarranted slur on the professional competence of the Press.

The journalists informed the Press Council that when the resolution to exclude the Press was moved, the seconder suggested that at the end of the meeting the Town Clerk should give a statement to the Press on the decisions arrived at. They complained that the resolution was wrongful because it did not comply with the Public Bodies (Admission to Meetings) Act, 1960. As eventually minuted, the resolution excluded the Press 'to enable the members and officers to have a detailed discussion on the Town Clerk's confidential report to members on future projects, including the proposed new swimming pool.' The journalists accepted that in this form the resolution complied with the Act but contended that the reason for the exclusion was not supported by what actually took place at the meeting in private when, according to the statement made to the Press the following day by the Town Clerk, the go-ahead was given by an overwhelming majority to the provision of a new swimming pool costing £528,000 and there was discussion on other projects costing several millions.

Both the journalists and the Town Clerk subsequently

issued statements expressing their points of view and there was a meeting between them which failed to resolve their differences.

The Town Clerk expressed to the Press Council the view that both the spirit and the letter of the statute had been observed. Though it did not appear in the minutes, the Council members who had decided that a special meeting of all the members of the Council should be called made it quite clear that they wanted the meeting in private and it was generally accepted that Press and public would be excluded. He conceded that the mover of the resolution to exclude the Press did not couch it in formal terms, but it was implicit that the purpose was to consider his, the Town Clerk's, confidential report. In his experience it seldom happened that members couched resolutions in formal terms. It was usually left to the Town Clerk to draft the appropriate resolution and this was done on this occasion for insertion in the minutes.

Mr. Crabtree said that the various projects to which references were made at the meeting in private were referred for attention to the appropriate committees so that each committee could take its own decision which would in due course be brought back to the Council for discussion in public. Having regard to the public interest in the proposed swimming pool, he was authorised to issue the statement to the Press the following day. In this he had said that the Council had indicated it would approve the committee concerned going ahead with the swimming pool.

The objection that in his remarks to the Borough Council he had cast a slur on the professional competence of the Press was put to Mr. Crabtree and he replied in a written statement 'I readily acknowledge that my words were unnecessary and uncalled for.' The Press Council stated that in view of that observation a finding was unnecessary.

The Council's statement continued: 'The second claim, that the public were wrongly excluded from the meeting, arises through the alleged failure of Cheltenham Borough Council to comply strictly with the statutory provision contained in the Public Bodies (Admission to Meetings) Act, 1960. The Press Council is satisfied that in moving the resolution that the public be excluded no reasons for exclusion were contained in the words used as is required by the statute. The fact that the Town Clerk recorded in the minutes what would have been a resolution complying with the statute did not remedy the defect.

'This is the second occasion within a year on which the Press Council has been asked to consider allegations of improper exclusion of the Press from council meetings.' In finding in the first instance that the Press had been improperly excluded, the Council announced that it had not accepted a claim that the fault was a technicality because it was of vital importance, firstly, that the resolution to exclude the Press should be debated in 'public' (as it was in the present instance) and, secondly, that the reasons should be stated in the resolution (as they were not in the present instance). The Council drew the attention of local authorities to the necessity for strict compliance with the statute.

From 15th annual report of the Press Council, pp. 104-106.

1. 7th annual report of the Press Council, pp. 29–30.
2. 11th annual report of the Press Council, pp. 42–43.

10 Attitudes to Secrecy in Central Government

'We think that the administrative process is surrounded by too much secrecy. The public interest would be better served if there were a greater amount of openness.'[1]

This is not a statement by an irate ratepayer's association or by a member of an aggrieved N.U.J. chapel but, in fact, by the full scale inquiry into the structure, recruitment and management of the Home Civil Service, appointed in February, 1966, and reporting in June, 1968. It is indicative of the growing feeling that, as a basic tenet of administration, secrecy is outmoded and contrary to the aspirations and desires of an increasingly better educated and more aware public.

The Fulton Committee went further:

> 'We welcome the trend in recent years towards wider and more open consultation before decisions are taken; and we welcome, too, the increasing provision of the detailed information on which decisions are made. Both should be carried much further; it is healthy for a democracy increasingly to press to be consulted and informed. *There are still too many occasions where information is unnecessarily withheld and consultation merely perfunctory*.'[2]

In spite of the strictures of the last sentence there is no doubt that central government is moving more and more towards the system of public consultation and participation.

An example of the increasingly open attitude in Whitehall can be found in the recent events in the esoteric field of official statistics. Following the wide-ranging debate on official statistics, especially financial statistics, during the last few years culminating in Fourth Report from the Estimates Committee in session 1966-67[3] there have been real efforts to bring up to date, to make more relevant and useful and to make more widely known the whole range of official statistics. Developments in this field have been chronicled in the Central Statistical Office's *Statistical News.* In a foreword to the first issue[4] of this publication the Prime Minister, the Rt. Hon. Harold Wilson, wrote:

'One of the features of modern decision-making is its reliance on statistics. This is true of the business world, of central and local government, and indeed all parts of society. As one consequence, the scale and complexity of government statistical systems has grown out of all recognition and it is now quite hard to keep up with all the new developments that take place.'

Subsequent issues of *Statistical News* have indicated the trends and changes in the statistics published by various government departments on which decisions are, in part at least, based. Since early 1968 there have been considerable changes in the form of published official statistics.

A further aspect of public participation has been the introduction of a new form of publication, the Green Paper. The Green Paper sets out for public discussion major ministerial proposals while they are still in their formative stages to allow comments to be made and changes to be made in policies in the light of reasoned and constructive criticism acceptable to the government of the day. Several Green Papers have already been published, notably 'Public Expenditure: A New Presentation' which dealt with a variety of suggestions for making the vexed subject of public spending more intelligible; 'The Task Ahead' dealing with the wider economic field; and, 'National Health Service: the Administrative Structure of the Medical and Related Services in England and Wales'.

This last Green Paper belied the argument that the ideas published are cut and dried and not capable of major change. In fact, the storm of controversy raised on its publication in July, 1968, has resulted in the publication of a further Green Paper, 'National Health Service: the Future Structure of the National Health Service' which contains some very much revised ideas.

It is regrettable that this trend towards the wider publication and more general usefulness of financial statistics and information has not been appreciated by M.P.s who, in a disgraceful display of apathy virtually boycotted the two day debate on the first of the new-style public expenditure White Papers at the end of January, 1970.[5]

In a summary-cum-declaration on the lifting of certain veils of secrecy and the provision of yet more information the Government published a White Paper, 'Information and the Public Interest'[6] which was presented to Parliament by the Prime Minister. It was unambiguous:

'The Government believe that there is scope for encouraging this trend towards publishing more material.'[7]

It was a little more cautious, however, on some of the Fulton Committee's recommendations:

'It does not follow, of course, that public consultation on tentative proposals is invariably the right course. It may result in slower decisions and slower action when prompt action is essential. Sometimes, too, conflicting views and conflicting interests are already well known. In such cases a prolonged period of consultation will merely impose delay without any compensating advantages.[8]

While in itself of little practical importance it is, nevertheless, symbolic that following a report of the Select Committee on Parliamentary Privilege[9] the Government recently decided to reverse the resolutions of the House of Commons dating from between 1694 and 1763 that maintained that publication of the reports of the proceedings of the House and its committees was illegal.[10]

In practice since the last quarter of the eighteenth century the House has not proceeded against reporters and, indeed, now it positively encourages publication of reports of its debates. It is reported that when, some years ago, Mr. George Wigg (now Lord Wigg) 'spyed strangers' in the Commons and the remainder of the day's business had to continue in the absence of the Press and public, the matters designed to carry the House through the day were rapidly concluded!

Apart from the increased pre-Budget information and the financial White Papers that look forward for two years at a time, 'Information and the Public Interest' listed *inter alia* some nineteen new or improved sources of information which illustrated the development of consultation and participation:

- Details of the financial objectives of nationalised industries contained in the 1967 White Paper, 'Economic and Financial Objectives of the Nationalised Industries';[11]
- The facts and considerations taken into account in forming the Government's fuel policy contained in the Ministry of Power's White Papers of 1965 and 1967;[12]
- The report of the Department of Employment and Productivity on the implications of a national minimum wage;
- The custom of publishing consultants' reports on the siting of new towns;
- Water Resources Board reports prior to major controversial water schemes;
- The publication of 'The Scottish Economy; a Plan for Expansion';[13]
- The publication of 'Wales; the Way Ahead';[14]
- The discussion of the White Paper, 'Social Work and the Community'[16] which led to the Social Work (Scotland) Act, 1968;
- The discussion of the White Papers, 'The Child, the Family and the Young Offender'[16] and 'Children in Trouble'[17] which led to the Children and Young Persons Act, 1969;
- The publication of a new 'Handbook of Statistics' by the Central Statistical Office;
- The publication of 'Social Trends' – a parallel publication to 'Economic Trends';
- The symposium 'Technological Innovation in Great Britain';
- The Ministry of Technology's series of pamphlets and the monthly bulletin for industry, 'New Technology';
- The Department of Education and Science digest, 'Science Bulletin';
- The new functional analysis of expenditure and

manpower in the Defence Department White Papers;

- The expanded Agriculture Department White Papers on the structure of forming and the implications for agriculture of the Common Market;
- The new series of press releases, 'Food Facts';
- The new monthly supplements to the Department of Education and Science annual report;
- The new quarterly, 'Health Trends', produced by the Department of Health and Social Security.

All these show conclusively that central government is endeavouring to practise what it preaches in wishing to see: '... more public explanation of administrative processes, a continuing trend towards more consultation before policy decisions are reached, and increasing participation by civil servants in explaining the work of Government to the public.'[18]

If these unimpeachable sentiments can be expressed, and practised, by central government why should they not be adopted by local government?

1. Report of the Fulton Committee on the Civil Service. June, 1968, para. 277.
2. *Ibid.* para. 278.
3. H.C. 246, 6th December, 1966.
4. May, 1968.
5. House of Commons Official Report. Vol. 714, col. 523–644, 21st January, 1970, and col. 723–837, 22nd January, 1970.
6. Cmnd. 4089, June, 1969.
7. *Ibid.*, para. 24.
8. *Ibid.*, para 14.
9. H.C. 34. 1st December, 1967.
10. The best known resolution, that of 3rd March, 1763, stated: 'That it is a high Indignity to, and a notorious Breach of, the Privilege of this House, for any News Writer, in Letters, or other Papers (as Minutes, or under any other Denomination) or for any Printer or Publisher of any printed Newspaper, of any Denomination, in Great Britain, Ireland, or any other Part of his Majesty's Dominions, to presume to insert in the said Letters or Papers, or to give therein any Account of the Debates, or other Proceedings of this House, or any Committee thereof, as well during the Recess, as the Sitting of Parliament; and that this House will proceed with the utmost Severity against such Offenders.'
11. Cmnd. 3437. November, 1967.
12. Cmnd. 2798 of October, 1965, and Cmnd. 3438 of November, 1967.
13. Cmnd. 2864. January, 1966.

14. Cmnd. 3334. July, 1967.
15. Cmnd. 3065. 1966.
16. Cmnd. 2742. August, 1965.
17. Cmnd. 3601. April, 1968.
18. 'Information and the Public Interest', Cmnd. 4089, para. 36.

11 The Ministers' Views

Since the passage of Mrs. Thatcher's Act there has been a remarkable unanimity of opinion on the part of successive Ministers of Housing and Local Government of *both* major parties. In May, 1961 Mr. Henry Brooke, (see p.17) the then Conservative Minister issued a circular[1] which, even now, is remarkable for its blunt plain speaking in an area where circumlocution is normal:

'It is important for the health of local government that the public should be able to obtain regular information and informed objective comment about the day-to-day work of the local authorities. Because most people get their information about local authorities' business from their local newspapers, the relationship between the authorities and the Press is of special importance. Both have a part to play.'[2]

Mr. Brooke, through the incisive medium of Miss (later Dame) Evelyn Sharp, made it clear that he was aware that most local authorities were, as the circular put it 'alive to their responsibilities' but he wanted to be sure that satisfactory arrangements were being made to ensure that the public would be informed.

'Minority voices,' he made it clear, 'should have the chance of expression.'[3]

But he was firm on certain points:—[4]

'Matters of real importance to the locality ought to be openly debated, unless there are compelling reasons against publicity ...'

'... reasons can be advanced to justify the conduct of a part of a local authority's business in private. They do not justify practices which result in the conduct of all the authority's business in private ...'

'... it is in the interests of good public relations that a clear indication should, wherever possible, be given of the reasons why it is considered that publicity would be prejudicial to the public interest. Only in exceptional cases, where an indication of the nature of the business would in itself be prejudicial to the public interest, should the explanation be simply in terms that the business is confidential.'

On the vexed question of publicity for planning applications he was equally firm:–

'... he would ask all authorities to consider whether enough is being done under their existing arrangements to secure appropriate publicity in cases of wide general interest.'[5]

Summarising, the Minister said: 'The essential thing in all these matters is that local authorities should keep the public and the Press fully informed, and should enable themselves to take account of public opinion in reaching their decisions. They may sometimes have to take unpopular decisions, even decisions to which there is strong local opposition. It is the more important that they should be seen to have acted in the knowledge of public opinion and that their reasons for their actions should be fully understood.'[6]

The passage of four years, a change of government and considerable changes in policy in other and related fields have not changed the tune on this subject and September, 1965 saw the new Minister, the Rt. Hon. Richard Crossman, O.B.E., M.P., speaking to the Association of Municipal Corporations Annual Conference at the Princess Theatre, Torquay:

'There are,' he said, 'lots of councils now which are not only allowing the Press into their full meetings and their committee meetings where they think it necessary, but who are also (much more important, I think) providing the Press with the agenda and the minutes without any embargo and with complete freedom of comment. That is the really important thing: to give the Press the material on which to make up their minds.'

Mr. Crossman then proceeded to destroy a myth that had gained a certain currency in the previous few years:

'Frankly, I have never heard of a council which, once it had the courage to co-operate fully with the Press in presenting the council to the electorate, has ever rescinded the charter of Press freedom in the town hall. I think this attitude to the Press is one of those acts of modernisation, like installing a fridge or putting central heating in the bedroom or a radio in the car. Once you have installed this rather exotic thing, it immediately becomes an essential part of civilised life without which you cannot live. Of course, it is true that each advance of civilisation adds to its complexities and the dire effects of a breakdown. Once you have a fridge, of course, it may not work, with disastrous results on the food inside it. Similarly, once you have the Press at the council, it may commit an indiscretion and it may write an incompetent story which infuriates you. These are the disadvantages of doing anything: that if you give somebody the chance to do a good job, you give them the chance to do a bad job as well. If you progress, you have that danger. Nevertheless, as I say, I do not think I know of a council which, having once tried this, ever went back on it. It is obviously something which, once you do it, works.

Indeed, I think the main concern of local government should be, not to keep the Press from prying into its affairs and from publishing them, but to try and persuade their local newspapers that local government is not as boring as they think. I think local government is a lively concern doing all sorts of lively things which any lively newspaper should want to cover. But that is not the impression which councils sometimes give to their newsmen. From outside, they look dull and musty, and you do not see the life in them. Your job, surely, is not to stop the Press prying, but to get more coverage from the Press, and better coverage.'

Turning to the question of the competence of journalists, he said:

'The journalist who is covering a local government story is often hard put to it – I am putting it moderately now – to explain to you the difference between gross and net rateable values, or to explain the formula on which council house subsidies are fixed. Or describe the difference between a town development and a new town. These seem to me the kind of standard questions you should ask a Press man before he becomes a local government reporter. May I say that if a sports reporter who hardly knew the difference between rugger and soccer were sent to cover an international there would be trouble: but there is less trouble if a man or woman with equal inadequacy is sent to dig into a very complicated and difficult story about local government.

'The main difficulty here is the general public. *We get the Press reports we deserve.* With a subject we are really interested in, the experts get to work, and they have to give a jolly good story. It is because the public would not stand an ignorant story about an international event that you get good stories. It is because the public cannot tell the difference between sense and nonsense in the council offices that you get the indifferent reporters. But, of course, that is no excuse for the Press, because the Press claims – and I passionately believe it should claim – to be the great educator and the great medium of adult education. The best way to educate the public about local government is to have Press reports which are slightly above the taste of the people, leading them on and encouraging them. I am making this plea to the Press: to see the importance of raising the standard of coverage of local government in the cause of local democracy.'

His strictures were not wholly acceptable to the Conference and Councillor W.L. Penny (at that time the Mayor of Blandford Forum) expressed a more cautious view:

'My feeling, as a representative of a small borough – and I am sure the feeling must be shared by many small boroughs – is that too much attention seems to be paid by the smaller local papers to the selling of newspapers. I do not know if that is to be the pattern of the future. For example, in recent years, we have had various things reported fully on television and in the newspapers – such things as: Should we allow women wrestlers in the Corn Exchange? Then, we had a slight infestation of rabbits on our recreation ground, and had to ask British Railways to gas their embankment. Again, it got full coverage in the local papers, and was reported on the radio and television in the West of England programmes. On the other hand, we spent £30,000 on improving our sewage works, and that got very little mention indeed. I should like to ask the Minister: Do you feel that the titillation of the public palate is to be the criterion on which the news value of the future must inevitably be dealt?'

Mr. Crossman's reply did not waver:

'There are many councils – I am sorry to say this – who do not want full Press co-operation and who do keep the Press out. Obviously, at a point where things are still confidential one has a perfect right to keep the Press from one's private meetings but if we want the public to appreciate what we are doing, we must want the Press to come into our town hall and share things with us. We must be willing to talk to them and, if I may say so, willing to trust them. We must trust them with 'off the record' information. There are places that do this, and there the relationship is generally excellent. Then it goes wrong because the good reporter is taken off and you get one bad incident which destroys the good relations between the council and the newspaper.'

Another four years passed and yet a further Minister of Housing & Local Government was in office. And still the policy had not changed. On 15th February, 1969 the Rt. Hon. Anthony Greenwood, M.P., addressing the Labour Party Local Government Conference at the Royal Hall, Harrogate explained that in his view two things are essential if local authorities are to convince the public that they are keeping pace with changing ideas. Firstly, they must be concerned with improving productivity and, secondly, '... far more of them must throw off the murky cloak of silence.'

Local authorities he said are responsible for over one quarter of public expenditure and 'the public have a right to know what councils are doing in their name and why they are doing it. Every councillor should search his conscience on the way his council operates the Public Bodies (Admission to Meetings) Act. The Act should be honoured in the spirit as well as in the letter.

Councils should see that the Press are informed about what is happening. If journalists are kept in ignorance and if decisions are taken behind closed doors which should be taken in public, councils have only themselves to blame if they have a hostile Press and an apathetic public.'

There can be few subjects in the field of local government affairs that over a period of eight years – a period virtually equally governed by Conservative and Labour governments – have produced such ministerial unanimity.

1. Ministry of Housing and Local Government Circular 21/61, reproduced in full at Appendix 4.
2. *Ibid.,* para. 3.
3. *Ibid.,* para 4.
4. *Ibid.,* paras. 6-9.
5. *Ibid.,* para. 14.
6. *Ibid.,* para. 16.

12 The Views of the Royal Commission and the Maud Committee

The Maud Committee and the Royal Commission both considered the relationship of local authorities with their public, especially through the medium of the Press and came to similar conclusions.

'In the relationship between local government and the public the function of the Press is, clearly, of immense importance,' stated the Royal Commission Report, 'The local Press gives a wide coverage of local government affairs. But the Press also suffers from the multiplicity of local authorities and the irrelevance of local government as at present organised.'[1]

The Commission thought that with hundreds of authorities to cover and with the confusion of responsibility (see page vii), it was difficult for attention to be focussed on real issues or to stir the public interest.

'In short,' stated the Commission, 'what is needed is a clarification of the local government system.'[2]

The Royal Commission noted that the Maud Committee had found both ignorance and indifference to local government by the public and put down this attitude to defects in the local government structure. The Maud Committee thoroughly examined the attitudes of the public to local government and of councillors to their public and the Tables in Appendix 6 reveal some of the attitudes found by the survey.

Tables 1 and 5 provide the fundamental figures of the authorities answering the questionnaire which admit the Press to committee meetings – other than education committees to which they are statutorily obliged to admit the Press. 10

per cent of those questioned admitted the Press to *all* their main committees; 40 per cent to some; and, 50 per cent to none. Of course, the 'some' to which 40 per cent admit the Press may mean anything from the road safety committee to the general purposes committee, or indeed any other committee of greater or lesser importance. In London the figures were generally worse than for the rest of the country but there are indications that this situation is changing.

The availability of agendas to the Press is covered by Tables 2 and 6 and here London is significantly more enlightened in allowing comment of committee recommendations before council meetings than the remainder of the country, particularly the county districts.

Tables 4 and 7 show quite clearly the difficult task that faces a newspaper if it is supplied with all, or even some, of the councillor's papers. In the largest county boroughs councillors in a typical month received an average of 642 foolscap sheets of reports, etc. Even the very large outer London Boroughs could not match this, with an average of 430 sheets per member.

One of the chief arguments against the admission of the public to committee meetings, namely their lack of interest seems to be borne out by the figures in Tables 3 and 8. In two-thirds of the authorities outside London no member of the public attended council meetings in the preceding twelve months while even at the most heavily attended meetings of the largest authorities, presumably on the most contentious occasions, no more than 60 attended and even that number was clearly unusual. The average in county districts where they had any attendances at all was about 4 or 5 and in the boroughs about 14. Certainly, this indicates little interest but the content of many council meetings in merely 'rubber-stamping' committee recommendations and the inadequate accommodation cannot be said to be attractive.

The Royal Commission research study, 'Community Attitudes Survey: England', indicated that:

'A local newspaper is, without doubt, one of the main sources of information for local news and, therefore, readership of the local Press may be a good indicator of people's interest in the community around them.'[3]

Tables 9-12 indicate some of the results found by the

Survey. They show that of all informants 87 per cent read at least one local newspaper, with this figure reaching as much as 90 per cent in the Metropolitan Boroughs. Perhaps even more startling is the figure of 53 per cent of people in conurbations who read two or more local newspapers.[4] More than half of the papers were weeklies although the provincial evening papers were high in the list (Table 10). Tables 11 and 12 deal with the number of newspapers regularly read.

In Volume 2 of the Report of the Committee on the Management of Local Government[5] the councillor's opinions were tested and in Tables 13 and 14 his views on the public knowledge of council affairs are summarised. Table 15 indicates that of all the things that might be done to raise the level of public interest councillors themselves thought that better coverage in the Press and the establishment of a public relations organisation are, respectively, the two most important possibilities.

A similar investigation of the electorate in Volume 3 of the Report[6] (Tables 16-24) showed that the prime source of information of local affairs, according to 68 per cent of those questioned, was the local Press. Nevertheless, only 25 per cent of those in county boroughs (and as few as 8 per cent in the metropolitan boroughs) had read any local council news in the local Press during the previous month.

Finally, as an indication of what has been happening and as a guide to what might be done in the future, Table 25 showed that 62 per cent of those who watch television and 78 per cent of those listening to radio in the twelve months before the survey had neither seen nor heard programmes on local government. The Maud Report noted the sensitivity of members toward Press reports and, 'the divergence of interests between the wish of the council to publicise its activities and to show the reasonableness of its decisions, and the need of the newspapers to pay heed to the readership appeal of their contents.'[7] Contrary to an often heard criticism the research report found no strong evidence of political bias in reporting local authority affairs – most of the criticisms refer to 'sensationalism, inaccuracies and bad coverage.'

Personal contacts are regarded as very important even on an informal basis between Press, members and officers.

The Maud Report recommended admission of the Press to committees of the type recommended elsewhere in the Report;[8] a partnership between councils and the Press in informing the public; appreciation of the difficulties of the Press; and, adequate facilities for Press representatives.[9]

The Royal Commission, building on the foundations of the Maud Report, and with additional evidence from its own research studies, was quite clear. While not prepared to recommend the exact machinery for consultation by the unitary authorities the appropriate guide lines are laid down for elected members and senior officers: 'Theirs will be the duty of ensuring that people are continuously aware of an authority's aims and efforts to achieve them, and that local officers take the public into their confidence. Theirs will also be the duty of making certain that the authority is kept aware of public opinion, both about general policies and individual services. They must deliberately establish and maintain working relationships with those responsible for newspapers, broadcasting and television, and seek their help in keeping open two-way communication between the public and their local governors.'[10]

1. Royal Commission on Local Government in England, Vol.1, para.98.
2. Royal Commission, para.99.
3. Page 65, para. (3).
4. Contrast these figures with Tables 22-24.
5. Entitled *The Local Government Councillor.*
6. Entitled *The Local Government Elector.*
7. Vol.1, para.452.
8. i.e. deliberative committees, see Vol.1, Chapter 3.
9. Volume 1, para. 462.
10. Royal Commission, Volume 1, para. 319.

13 People and Planning the Skeffington Report

Over the years secrecy about planning decisions coupled with a feeling of helplessness on the part of the average citizen has been a bone of contention and the pressure for change increased until in March, 1968, a Committee was appointed under the chairmanship of Mr. Arthur Skeffington, M.P.: 'to consider and report on the best methods, including publicity, of securing the participation of the public at the formative stage in the meeting of development plans for their area.'

The report of the Committee, 'People and Planning',[1] was published in October, 1969, and dealt with a variety of involvement techniques. Time and again, however, the Committee referred to the use that might, and should, be made of the Press. Discussing the area of the debate surrounding public participation the Committee stated:

> 'Many of the submissions we received pressed for special consideration to be given to the contributor's particular interest but common themes ran through several. They included, for example, more education in planning matters; far better access to, and a wider distribution of, information; for a statutory right of consultation by local amenity societies or for their representations to be co-opted to the planning committees; *for planning committees to be open to the Press;* and, for a closer link between physical planning and social welfare work.'[2]

The Committee states that: 'Participation is dependant upon an adequate supply of information to the public'[3] and they were sure that the local Press provided a vital means of publicity – read, they allege, by 90 per cent of the adult population.[4] A regular flow of information to the Press is an essential requirement[5] including regular meetings between the planning department and the local Press at such intervals that any news presented is still fresh.

In particular, when a major planning document is to be presented to the local residents the regular flow of information is particularly necessary although there is a chance of unbalanced reporting if care is not taken to ensure that any such plans are properly presented. Suitably qualified reporters are an essential part of this process.[6]

Local planning authorities are asked to ensure that all documents are issued well in advance with any embargo on publication date long enough to allow the newspaper staff to do a proper job.[7] As the committee stated:

> 'If publicity is to enable the public to contribute, planning news ought to be issued in time for comment in advance of a final decision.'[8]

Regular briefings, the non-attributable statement, the sending of copies of major advertisements to the local editor and planning correspondent as well as to the advertising manager are all recommended as part of the overall techniques of involvement.

The committee was careful, however, to emphasise that all the efforts should not have to emanate from the local authorities. It hoped that editors would see that material supplied is reported objectively and responsibly.[9] But, 'this does not mean that argument should be avoided.'

Indeed, this very argument may well serve to stir the public interest. The planning department is entitled to expect constructive reporting but, on the other hand, it 'must not be unduly touchy or defensive about public criticism or refuse to become involved in public argument.'[10]

The Committee draws attention to the increase of the significance of local radio and suggests that planning matters might well stimulate public discussion on the radio just as well as in newspapers.[11]

> 'We recommend that local planning authorities should consider providing facilities for the broadcasting of council debates on the big planning decisions.'[12]

One powerful argument that the Committee mentions, almost in passing, is that the public have a way of not reading statutory notices and for this reason should be publicised by other means than the straight advertisement.

Two significant points emerge from the Skeffington Report. Firstly, there is a need for local authorities to make a more detailed and imaginative use of the Press resources in order to deal with planning matters and, secondly, local authorities already make considerable use of the local Press, if only because they are statutorily obliged to use them for advertising. It seems that, if the committee's recommendations are adopted, the local Press should cease merely to be a vehicle for dull, uniformative statutory advertisements and should, instead, be the proper basis of a two-way flow of information and comment on planning matters.

1. A new-style cartoon-illustrated document.
2. 'People and Planning', para. 16. Author's italics.
3. *Ibid.*, para.100.
4. *Ibid.*, para. 104.
5. *Ibid.*, para. 106.
6. *Ibid.*, para. 108.
7. *Ibid.*, para. 109.
8. *Ibid.*, para. 109.
9. *Ibid.*, para. 112.
10. *Ibid.*, para. 112.
11. *Ibid.*, para. 112.
12. *Ibid.*, para. 120.

14 Local Radio

While the dictionary definition of 'the Press' is confined, in general terms, to newspapers and magazines there is little doubt that radio and television come these days within the same category as part of the network of communications media.

At the present time the number of local authorities having practical experience of broadcasting and television appearances is comparatively small. Apart from the larger metropolitan authorities, such as the Greater London and Birmingham City Councils, *regular* broadcasting and television experience is even rarer. Such experience as the majority of the others have had has probably been the result of some once-and-for-all encounter arising from a particularly interesting or unusual local event that might be of national or regional interest. It might, unfortunately, have resulted from some alleged scandal about which the television producers sought to make a newsworthy story.

It is, therefore, hardly surprising that only one paragraph[1] in Volume 5 of the Report of the Committee on Management of Local Government is devoted to broadcasting and television and the comments in that paragraph are confined to some generalities about resentment felt by certain councillors and officers that they require the permission of the council chairman before making a television appearance.

But this situation is changing at this very moment. In November, 1967 the first of eight B.B.C. local radio stations began to broadcast in an experiment watched with anxiety by both the B.B.C. and the Government[2] and viewed with suspicion by commercial broadcasting interests.

Each station is of relatively low power and cannot be heard far outside the area of the particular town on which it is centred. Over half of the recurring expenditure of local radio stations during the experimental period has come from local sources, mainly from local authorities, and although the B.B.C. have said:

'This method of financing has not brought with it any unusual pressures and has created no special problems.'[3] There is a strong difference of opinion as to the success of this particular means of providing the necessary day-to-day money for the scheme.

The assistant editor of the *Municipal Review* was not so sanguine. Having visited Stoke-on-Trent and Brighton radio stations she wrote:

'Has the local radio experiment been a success? I think Mr. Blake's (Deputy Town Clerk of Brighton) opinion is that shared by all authorities who have a radio station within their borough's boundaries. 'The service is a success, the lamentable failure is in the financing'.'[4]

Nevertheless, whatever the differences of opinion, Mr. John Stonehouse, the then Postmaster-General,[5] announced that the experiment had clearly been a success and the local radio system would be improved by the establishment of 40 local stations. 20, including the eight experimental stations, have already been announced and they will serve 70 per cent of the population of England. The other 20 would be set up in Scotland and Wales as well as England and about 90 per cent of the population would then be able to receive their programmes. The stations were scheduled to be established by 1974 and each will cost about £60,000 to establish and up to £100,000 a year in expenses,[6] but the General Election brought inevitable change and the new Government has announced that commercial local radio will be introduced in due time.

The variety of subjects covered by local radio stations is every bit as wide as the national coverage by Radios 2 and 4 – wider in that certain purely local, purely parochial matters that are unsuitable for national networks are naturally suited to the local station. One of the largest potential wells of material for local radio stations – as with local newspapers –

is the local authority and the eight experimental stations have broadcast scores of hours of local government material in the form of news items, announcements and features. Councillors and officers have become part of the regular cast of performers and the more aware members of the authorities have been careful to ensure their availability and their co-operation with this medium which for practical purposes is brand new.

There have been problems such as those revealed in the *Municipal Journal*[7] where it was said that at least one local radio manager was having trouble with election agents who were not allowing their candidates to broadcast – for a number of reasons. One agent would not let his candidate broadcast as it would have been revealed that the candidate was 86 years old!

Furthermore, under the Representation of the People Act, unless *all* the candidates for a chosen ward were prepared to take part in a broadcast then *none* of them could do so. Political agents preferred, so the article said, to pre-select words and candidates.

But in spite of these tribulations there is no doubt that in the next four or five years local radio will become a serious news-gathering rival to the local Press over most of the country. The co-operation required for effective local authority-Press relations should be extended to include the reporters of local radio stations and, in anticipation of their arrival, local councils should begin to make adequate arrangements for them including, perhaps, a suitable interview room and, after consultations, certain other technical requirements.

And after local radio there will doubtless be, in due course, local television ...

1. Chapter 17, para. 27.
2. The experimental stations are Radios Leicester, Sheffield, Merseyside, Nottingham, Brighton, Stoke-on-Trent, Leeds and Durham.
3. *This is Local Radio*. Hugh Pierce. B.B.C. Local Radio Development Manager.
4. *Local Radio – has it worked?* Lee Brown. Municipal Review.
5. Later Minister of Posts and Telecommunications.
6. House of Commons Official Report. Vol.792, col.1517. 3rd December, 1969.
7. 17th May, 1968, p. 1170.

15 What is being done

It will be seen from previous Chapters that the contest (if that is the correct word) between the two sides has swayed first one way and then the other. Because each local authority can take its own decision and can, of course, change its mind it is difficult to establish a rational pattern and all any observer can do is to quote the few surveys that have been conducted. The surveys by Dr. Dilys Hill, *The Times* and by Margaret Harrison and Alan Norton[1] for the Maud Committee have already been mentioned.

Other, smaller, surveys have been undertaken from time to time by individuals, by newspapers and, occasionally, by interested organisations. For instance, in 1967 the Institute of Journalists gathered information about local authority-Press relations in the Essex area, obtaining its information from journalists in the district, and as a result of its findings wrote to the clerks of various councils in an endeavour to better those relations.

The Institute, which has a dual membership arrangement with the National Union of Journalists, acts on behalf of both bodies on professional – as distinct from trade union – questions. It has always claimed to be a prime mover in the betterment of relations between local councils and their newspapers. To this end it is at present negotiating, with the Local Government Information Office, a code of conduct designed to be adopted by local authorities and the newspapers operating in their areas.

A Local Government Information Office pamphlet, 'Public Relations and Communication', states:

'It is essential the electorate, and even those who

are not yet able to vote, are kept well informed. They should be well informed because it is the moral duty of those of us who help to run democracy to ensure that the fullest information is always available. Such policy can only encourage enthusiasm, and inculcate in more people the desire to play a part in making each community a better place in which to live.'

The L.G.I.O. in common with the Institute of Journalists believe that keeping the electorate informed means more than just giving them a mass of detail – they must be given information early enough and fully enough for public opinion, including minority views, to be expressed and to pay its proper part in policy-making.

To this end they have drawn up a six point guide which covers most of the points at issue. This guide, which is reproduced below, has been agreed with and endorsed by the local authority associations and is being published at about the time that this book appears.

The snag is that existing legislation has been unable to keep recalcitrant local authorities in line and one can hardly be more sanguine about a purely voluntary code of conduct. If the guidance was followed in the spirit and the letter there might not be any need for additional legislation, but history does not encourage one to be optimistic.

L.G.I.O. – Institute of Journalists Recommended Guidance on the issue of information by bona fide journalists.

Outline Procedure

1. Where there is no official public relations officer, there should be someone to act as a liaison officer with Press, television and radio representatives. Normally this is the Clerk, though he may delegate these duties to an official senior enough to satisfy the requirements suggested below for a public relations officer.
Where the council has appointed a public relations officer, he should be of sufficient standing and seniority to inspire both the confidence and the respect of his

colleagues and the elected representatives and the Press. He is an expert serving other experts.

It is suggested that the council should have a definite policy regarding Press information and that all chief officers and their departments should be briefed as to the facilities that should be given to the Press in the search for information.

The liaison officer should be responsible for issuing Press information of all minor events, dates of meetings and advance information when there is likely to be an important policy statement or news item pending. On more major matters the Press representatives should have access to the Town Clerk or Clerk and other chief officers, and as necessary, to the chairman of the authority and committee chairmen, though they will recognise that it is impractical for members and senior officers to devote a large part of their time to dealing with Press enquiries and that whilst local authorities are anxious to co-operate with the Press, they cannot always answer Press enquiries immediately upon demand.

2. Attention is drawn to Circular 21/61 issued by the Ministry of Housing and Local Government as guidance to the Public Bodies (Admission to Meetings) Act, 1960, which provides that meetings of local authorities and certain committees should be open to the public. Committees governed by the Act include joint committees of two or more local authorities, education committees, and divisional executives and committees whose members include all members of the authority. Admission of the Press to committees to which the Act does not apply is a question for each local authority to decide, and they may properly take into account the extent of the confidentiality of the committee business under consideration.

3. If committees are not open to the Press probably the most satisfactory alternative will be for as much information as can properly be published to be released at the earliest possible moment. Authorities will, from local experience, judge the best method of releasing information – i.e. whether by Press conference or Press release – and in making arrangements will make due

allowance for the publication times of different papers and the timing of television and radio news and magazine programmes, so that there can be no complaint that one particular medium has continual advantage over others. This is specially important when major issues are to be announced or discussed. The Press conference technique should not be operated to the disadvantage of an individual reporter who has shown initiative by obtaining advance information from other sources. Care should be taken that agendas and reports adequately explain the nature of the business; if it can only be fully understood by reference to plans or models, for example, which cannot be circulated, they should be made available for inspection by the Press. Information about staff and policy matters should be issued by local authorities as necessary.

4. Use may also be made of the informal Press conference to explain problems and policy matters, sometimes off-the-record. Good Press relations are helped if authorities state – if necessary 'off-the-record' the reasons for withholding information. It is recognised that on a minority of occasions local authorities need to withhold information in the public interest and not because there is something to hide.

5. Similarly when the business of a meeting normally open to the Press is conducted in private an explanation should be given by the local authority of why publicity would be harmful. There should be only rare occasions when even an explanation would be prejudicial to the public interest and has to be confined to the statement that the business is confidential. By these means mutual respect and trust will be fostered.

6. Issue of information should be ragarded as a matter of routine and an important part of the management policy of the council and should be interfered with only for the most compelling reasons of public interest or council efficiency. Adverse comment on the council or mis-reporting of council activities in any section of the Press are not adequate reasons. Complaints, difficulties and misunderstandings should be taken up initially with the newspapers concerned. If no satis-

factory settlement is reached the complaints may be referred to the appropriate professional bodies, or, in the ultimate, the Press Council. Such difficulties would often be avoided, however, if local authorities took care to provide, and journalists to use, facilities for the checking of facts in any particular instance in which the Press or other medium of information proposed to be critical of local government policy. Journalists should have regard to delays which may occur if they approach members and officers at times of the day when they cannot refer to documents.

1. See pages 25, 28 and 73-76.

16 Some Suggestions

This book has been concerned with local authority – Press relations over the past sixty or so years but not simply as a historical record. Rather, the model of the previous decades should indicate the way in which these relations should, or should not, move in the coming years.

All the evidence indicates that local authorities must of necessity grow more remote as they become bigger and more powerful in the coming years. However much governments may rail against cynics and whatever safeguards both they and the Royal Commissions may try to build into the new system the fact is that in most cases the centre of local government power is to be removed one or perhaps two stages further away from the citizen. When bureaucratic bodies become large and remote, some form of safeguard must be established to protect the public. This protection is not necessarily against the machinations of evil-minded megalomaniacs but rather against the indifference and unintentional inhumanity of the mechanised, computerised department.

It is true that some additional steps are contemplated to deal with complaints of maladministration in local government. For instance on 22nd July, 1969 the Prime Minister announced to the House of Commons[1] that the Government accepted in principle that an ombudsman system should be established by law to investigate any such complaints:

'The activities of local authorities impinge upon the daily life of the citizens directly and over a wide range and the introduction of a system analogous to that of the

Parliamentary Commissioner into the local government sphere would be a major extension of the citizen's right to seek redress.'

In the course of answering questions on his statement Mr. Wilson made the point:

'If the trend is to be to a smaller number of large local authorities, that means that there will be fewer local councillors[2] with executive responsibility in the fields that most touch the citizen and general public, and that strengthens the case for getting on with the proposals.'

However, the local ombudsman system when it is eventually established is to work on a similar basis to that of the Parliamentary Commissioner for Administration and complaints will be routed through councillors.[3] Our ubiquitous cynic might be forgiven for asking who is to act as watchdog on the councillors. One answer was provided by the Royal Commission on Tribunals of Inquiry[4] who stated categorically:

'The Press is a watchdog of our liberties. They often reveal matters which should be disclosed in the public interest.'[5]

It is not claimed that the press is the only watchdog of our liberties but it is certainly a convenient, cheap and often effective method of throwing light into dark corners.

The local newspaper: '... is the link between electors and elected; through its reports justice must manifestly be seen to be done, not only in Courts of Law but by agents of power everywhere. It is the cement that holds local democracy together ...'[6]

The Social Survey undertaken for the Maud Committee on Management in Local Government[7] showed that 79 per cent of the sample questioned claimed to read their local newspaper regularly and 68 per cent said that local happenings were brought to their attention through the local Press. Indeed very many local residents would know nothing of their council's activities were it not for the local Press – this is a situation that may change significantly in the next few years with the advent of local radio and, even, local television, but this does not detract from the argument, radio and television interviewers and journalists being included in the generic term, Press, for the purposes of this book (see also Chapter 14).

Local authorities simply cannot afford to ignore their local Press and, going even further, they cannot afford to ignore the need constantly to improve, up-date and streamline their co-operation with local newspapers.

Conversely, no local newspaperman would be doing his duty if he ignored his local authority as a rich source of public interest but in doing so he must ensure, in the public interest, a high standard of integrity and journalistic competence in the treatment of local government items in his columns.

To achieve this end and, where necessary, to put the houses of all those concerned in order the following recommendations are made:

- Strengthen the Public Bodies (Admission to Meetings) Act, 1960.
- Ensure that any exclusion of the Press from committee meetings is fully, and where possible, publicly justified.
- Make sanctions on offending local authorities simpler and more effective.
- Establish an advisory committee on Press and public relations to advise the Minister and to make periodic recommendations to local authorities and the Press.
- Devise a short course of training in local government procedures for new local reporters.
- Produce a manual of local authority functions for reporters.
- Establish occasional courses in Press and public relations for local authority members.

The detailed proposals are as follows:

1. *Strengthen the Public Bodies (Admission to Meetings) Act, 1960.*

The existing Act should be amended to permit the Press to attend *all* committee meetings of the local authority as of right with the saving that councils may still require the Press to withdraw in certain circumstances when publicity might be prejudicial to the public interest because of the confidential nature of the business to be transacted. There is only one possible exemption to this rule and that is in the case of the policy committee. The Maud Committee on the Management of Local Government recommended[8] that each local authority should establish a 'management board', or policy committee. One of the advantages of this system, which is being slowly adopted in an increasing number of authorities, is to enable officers to be present at what is really the equivalent, in politically controlled authorities, of the party 'caucus' meeting. To admit the Press to such a meeting would drive the real policy-making back into the caucus thus destroying much of the purpose of establishing a policy committee. Realistic observers are agreed that all the new unitary and metropolitan authorities will be politically controlled and, thus, this will be an important consideration. In strengthening the Public Bodies (Admission to Meetings) Act the policy committee will need to be carefully defined in order not to provide a new loophole.

2. *Justification.* There should be a statutory obligation on all local authorities excluding the Press from committee meetings under the exception mentioned above, where their admission might be prejudicial to the public interest, to make a public justification of the exclusion unless the justification itself might prove to be prejudicial. If the latter is the case then an entry should be made in a special confidential register detailing the full circumstances why secrecy had been felt desirable. This register would be inspected annually by the Minister or, perhaps, the area ombudsman, when his office is established, to ensure that the spirit as well as the letter of the law is being observed.

3. *Sanctions.* The sanctions imposed on an offending local authority should be made more effective. It is suggested that the present 'relator' action at the suit of the Attorney General for an injunction or order of *mandamus* should be abandoned as being incomprehensible to the man-in-the-street and so tied about with red-tape as to be practically unworkable.[9] In its place should be a simple action in the High Court to obtain an injunction to prevent the local authority from

discussing either the matter over which the Press was excluded or related matters or matters arising in secret. The cost of a successful action should be surcharged on the members of the authority.

4. *Advisory committee.* The Minister of Housing and Local Government is advised by a number of distinguished committees on various aspects of his work. At the time of writing there are over 30 of these committees advising on everything from the design of underground pipe sewers to footpaths; from allotments to refuse disposal. It is proposed that an advisory committee on similar lines and composed of distinguished Press, public relations and local authority representatives be established to give continuous advice to the Minister and to the local authorities and the Press

5. *Training courses for journalists.* The Local Government Training Board in conjunction with the Institute of Journalists, or the National Union of Journalists, should devise a short, adaptable training course for young journalists concentrating on practical aspects of the reporting of local authorities' affairs. The course should be capable of adaptation by individual local authorities and should include such things as tours of local authority departments, meetings with key employees and with individual councillors and the attendance in a non-reporting capacity at committee and council meetings with a suitably informed council officer to explain the more obscure points.

6. *Manual.* As a complement to the practical course recommended at (5) above it is recommended that the Local Government Information Office should produce a manual for journalists detailing local government functions, some of the problems that face councillors and sources of information from which journalists may complete their background knowledge of local government. It should be possible for a section of the manual to be completed, and up-dated, by individual local authorities with such things as local statistics, financial details and other useful but strictly local information.

7. *Public relations.* It is to be hoped that when the new unitary authorities are established there will be provision on the staff of each for a public relations officer but even if this should be the case there will still be room for occasional courses or conferences for local authority members on the importance of adequate local authority-Press relations at which the problems facing both councillors and journalists are aired and solutions propounded and discussed.

The opportunity to introduce legislation on these lines may well occur in the 1971-72 session of Parliament when the Government is thought likely to introduce its Bill to reform local government in England. While such a Bill will be regarded with suspicion, even disfavour, by many people interested in local government affairs any means of mitigating fears of remoteness, bureaucracy and inhumanity will be welcomed. Perhaps these suggestions will form a small part of that mitigation.

1. House of Commons Debates. Vol.787, col.1501.

2. Probably not more than 7,000 in the main authorities, as opposed to 32,000 in existing authorities, excluding parishes, per Mr. Crosland (H.C. Debates, 18th February, 1970, Vol. 796, col. 435).

3. Reform of Local Government in England. Cmnd. 4276, para. 85. The present suggestion is for 10 or more Commissioners each working independently in a particular part of the country.

4. Cmnd. 3121. November, 1966.

5. *Ibid.,* para. 124.

6. Hervey Benham, *Two Cheers for the Town Hall*, 1964, p. 251.

7. Volume 5, 'Local Government Administration in England & Wales', p. 424. A survey undertaken by Research Services Ltd. as part of the Community Attitudes Survey: England (Research Study No. 9) for the Royal Commission and incorporating certain questions derived from the 'Local Government Elector' Survey (carried out by the Government Social Survey) in fact showed that 87 per cent of all informants regularly read one local newspaper and as many as 36 per cent read two or more. In certain areas these figures rose to 90 per cent and 53 per cent respectively.

8. *Op. cit.* para. 168.

9. See *Tynemouth Corporation* v. *Attorney-General* (1899) A.C. 293. The relator is responsible for costs; see *Attorney-General* v. *Poole Corporation* (1938) Ch. 23, C.A.

Bibliography

Sources are mentioned under the chapter in which they first appear.

Introduction

Report of the Committee on Management in Local Government. March, 1967.
Local Government in Wales. Cmnd. 3340. July, 1967.
Royal Commission on Local Government in England. Cmnd. 4040. June, 1969.
Royal Commission on Local Government in Scotland. Cmnd. 4150. September, 1969.
Reform of Local Government in England. Cmmd. 4276. February, 1970.
Royal Commission on Local Government in Greater London, 1957-60. Cmnd. 1164. October, 1960.

Chapter 1

Various national, provincial and local newspapers 1965-1970.

Chapter 2

Tenby Corporation v. Mason (1908) Ch. 561.

Chapters 3 and 4

Public Bodies (Admission of Press) Bill. Bill 60. 28th January, 1949.
Public Bodies (Admission of the Press to Meetings) Bill. Bill 172. 1st August, 1956.

Public Bodies (Admission of the Press to Meetings) Bill, later amended to Public Bodies (Admission to Meetings) Bill. Bill 18. 11th November, 1959.
H.C. Debates Vol. 616. 5th February, 1960.
H.C. Debates Vol. 623. 13th May, 1960.
Public Bodies (Admission to Meetings) Bill. Reports of Standing Committee D. April, 1960.
The M.P.'s Chart. Andrew Roth. Parliamentary Profile Services Ltd. 1966-67.

Chapter 5

U.D.C.A. Memorandum on Practical Points. April 1961.
A.M.C. Report (General Purposes Committee) 5/1961. 1st June 1961.
New Law and Practice of Parish Administration. Charles Arnold-Baker. Longcross Press. 1966.

Chapter 6

H.C. Debates Vol. 616.
The Times, various dates in December, 1961, and January, 1963.
The Council and the Press. A.J. Beith. New Society. 9th September, 1965.
Report of the Bognor Regis Inquiry. Ministry of Housing and Local Government, 1965.
Censorship No. 6. Spring, 1966.
Local Authorities and the Press. Local Government Chronicle. 4th and 11th December, 1965.
Participating in Local Affairs. Dr. Dilys Hill. Penguin Books, 1970.
Local Council Digest. Special Political Supplement. 6th April, 1968.
Local Government Reform in England. Labour Party. September 1969.
Principles for Local Government Reform in England. Labour Party. December 1969.

Chapter 7

Blyth News/Advertiser, various dates 1969 and 1970.

The Journal, Newcastle, various dates 1969 and 1970.
Guide to the Northumberland Coast. Ward Lock & Co. Ltd.
H.C. Written Answer, 18th November 1969. Vol. 791, col. 254.

Chapters 8 and 9

7th to 15th Annual Reports of the Press Council.

Chapter 10

Report of the Fulton Committee on the Civil Service. June, 1968.
Fourth Report of the Estimates Committee (Session 1966-67). H.C. 246. 6th December, 1966.
Statistical News. C.S.O. May, 1968.
H.C. Debates. Vol. 714.
Information and the Public Interest. Cmnd. 4089. June, 1969.
Report of the Select Committee on Parliamentary Privilege. H.C.34. 1st December, 1967.

Chapter 11

Ministry of Housing and Local Government Circular 21/61.
A.M.C. Conference Report 1965.

Chapter 12

Royal Commission on Local Government in England, Volume 1.
Committee on Management of Local Government, Volume 2, 'The Local Government Councillor'.
Committee on Management of Local Government, Volume 3, 'The Local Government Elector'.
Royal Commission Research Study No. 9, 'Community Attitudes: England'.

Chapter 13

People and Planning. Report of the Skeffington Committee. Ministry of Housing and Local Government. October, 1969.

Chapter 14

This is Local Radio. Hugh Pierce, B.B.C. Local Radio Development Manager. B.B.C. Publications. 1968.
'Local Radio – has it worked?' Lee Brown. Municipal Review.
H.C. Debates Vol. 792.

Chapter 15

'Public Relations and Communications'. Local Government Information Office.

Chapter 16

H.C. Debates Vol. 787.
Hervey Benham, *Two Cheers for the Town Hall,* Hutchinson. 1964.
Tynemouth Corporation v. Attorney-General, (1899) A.C. 293.
Attorney-General v. Poole Corporation, (1938) Ch. 23, C.A.

List of Appendices

1. Local Authorities (Admission of the Press to Meetings) Act, 1908
2. Public Bodies (Admission to Meetings) Act, 1960
3. Local Government Act, 1933, Sch. 3, Part IV, para. 1.
4. Ministry of Housing & Local Government Circular 21/61.
5. Authorities known to admit the press to some or all major committees.
6. Tables:

   (1) Admission of Press to committee meetings.
   (2) Availability of agendas
   (3) Attendance by public at council meetings.
   (4) Quantity of paper circulated to elected members.
   (5) – (8) as (1) – (4) for London Boroughs.
   (9) Readership of local newspapers.
   (10) Types of local newspapers read.
   (11) Number of local newspapers read.
   (12) Number of local newspapers read, by status and education.
   (13) Councillors' views – by age.

APPENDIX I.

THE LOCAL AUTHORITIES (ADMISSION OF THE PRESS TO MEETINGS) ACT, 1908

(8 Edw. 7 c.34)

An Act to provide for the Admission of Representatives of the Press to the Meetings of certain Local Authorities.

1. Representatives of the press to be admitted to the meetings of a local authority subject to a proviso. – Representatives of the press shall be admitted to the meetings of every local authority: Provided that a local authority may temporarily exclude such representatives from a meeting as often as may be desirable at any meeting when, in the opinion of a majority of the members of the local authority present at such meeting, expressed by resolution, in view of the special nature of the business then being dealt with or about to be dealt with, such exclusion is advisable in the public interest.

2. Definitions. – For the purposes of this Act the expression 'local authority' means –

(a) A council of a county, county borough, borough (including a metropolitan borough), urban district, rural district, or parish, and a joint committee or joint board of any two or more such councils to which any of the powers or duties of the appointing councils may have been transferred or delegated under the provisions of any Act of Parliament or Provisional Order; and a parish meeting under the provisions of the Local Government Act, 1894;

(b) An education committee and a joint education committee, established under section seventeen of the Education Act, 1902, so far as respects any acts or proceedings which are not required to be submitted to the council or councils for its or their approval;

(c) A board of guardians and a joint committee

constituted in pursuance of section eight of the Poor Law Act, 1879, and the board of management of any school or asylum district formed under any of the Acts relating to the relief of the poor;

(d) A central body and a distress committee under the Unemployed Workmen Act, 1905;

(e) The Metropolitan Water Board and a joint water board constituted under the provisions of any Act of Parliament or Provisional Order;

(f) Any other local body which has, or may hereafter have, the power to make a rate.

The expression 'rate' means a rate the proceeds of which are applicable to public local purposes, and leviable on the basis of an assessment in respect of property, and includes any sum which, though obtained in the first instance by a precept, certificate, or other document requiring payment from some authority or officer, is or can be ultimately raised out of a rate.

The expression 'representatives of the press' means duly accredited representatives of newspapers and duly accredited representatives of news agencies which systematically carry on the business of selling and supplying reports and information to newspapers.

3. Saving for committee meetings. – This Act shall not extend to any meeting of a committee of a local authority, as defined for the purposes of this Act, unless the committee is itself such an authority.

4. Power of committee. – Nothing in this Act shall be construed so as to prohibit a committee of a local authority from admitting representatives of the press to its meetings.

5. Admission of the public. – Nothing in this Act shall be construed so as to prohibit a local authority from admitting the public to its meetings.

6. (Applies to Scotland)

7., Short title and extent. – (1) This Act may be cited as the Local Authorities (Admission of the Press to Meetings) Act, 1908.

(2) This Act shall not extend to Ireland.

APPENDIX 2.

THE PUBLIC BODIES (ADMISSION TO MEETINGS) ACT, 1960

(8 & 9 Eliz. 2 c.67)

ARRANGEMENT OF SECTIONS

Section.

An Act to provide for the admission of representatives of the press and other members of the public to the meetings of certain bodies exercising public functions.

1. *Admission of public to meetings of local authorities and other bodies.* – (1) Subject to subsection (2) below, any meetings of a local authority or other body exercising public functions, being an authority or other body to which this Act applies, shall be open to the public.

(2) A body may, by resolution, exclude the public from a meeting (whether during the whole or part of the proceedings) whenever publicity would be prejudicial to the public interest by reason of the confidential nature of the business to be transacted or for other special reasons stated in the resolution and arising from the nature of that business or of the proceedings; and where such a resolution is passed, this Act shall not require the meeting to be open to the public during proceedings to which the resolution applies.

(3) A body may under subsection (2) above treat the need to receive or consider recommendations or advice from sources other than members, committees or sub-committees of the body as a special reason why publicity would be prejudicial to the public interest, without regard to the subject or purport of the recommendations or advice; but the making by this subsection of express provision for that case shall not be taken to restrict the generality of subsection (2) above in relation to other cases (including in particular cases where the report of a committee or sub-committee of the body is of a confidential nature).

(4) Where a meeting of a body is required by this Act to be open to the public during the proceedings or any part of them, the following provisions shall apply, that is to say, –

(a) public notice of the time and place of the meeting shall be given by posting it at the offices of the body (or, if the body has no offices, then in some central and conspicuous place in the area with which it is concerned) three clear days at least before the meeting or, if the meeting is convened at shorter notice, then at the time it is convened;

(b) there shall, on request and on payment of postage or other necessary charge for transmission, be supplied for the benefit of any newspaper a copy of the agenda for the meeting as supplied to members of the body (but excluding, if thought fit, any item during which the meeting is likely not to be open to the public), together with such further statements or particulars, if any, as are necessary to indicate the nature of the items included or, if thought fit in the case of any item, with copies of any reports or other documents supplied to members of the body in connection with the item;

(c) while the meeting is open to the public, the body shall not have power to exclude members of the public from the meeting and duly accredited representatives of newspapers attending for the purpose of reporting the proceedings for those newspapers shall, so far as practicable, be afforded reasonable facilities for taking their report and, unless the meeting is held in premises not belonging to the body or not on the telephone, for telephoning the report at their own expense.

(5) Where a meeting of a body is required by this Act to be open to the public during the proceedings or any part of them, and there is supplied to a member of the public attending the meeting, or in pursuance of paragraph (b) of subsection (4) above there is supplied for the benefit of a newspaper, any such copy of the agenda as is mentioned in that paragraph, with or without further statements or particulars for the purpose of indicating the nature of any item included in that agenda, the publication thereby of any defamatory matter contained in the agenda or in the further statement or particulars shall be privileged, unless the publication is proved to be made with malice.

(6) When a body to which this Act applies resolves itself into committee, the proceedings in committee shall for the purpose of this Act be treated as forming part of the proceedings of the body at the meeting.

(7) Any reference in this section to a newspaper shall apply also to a news agency which systematically carries on the business of selling and supplying reports or information to newspapers, and to any organisation which is systematically engaged in collecting news for sound or television broadcasts; but nothing in this section shall require a body to permit the taking of photographs of any proceedings, or the use of any means to enable persons not present to see or hear any proceedings (whether at the time or later), or the making of any oral report on any proceedings as they take place.

(8) The provisions of this section shall be without prejudice to any power of exclusion to suppress or prevent disorderly conduct or other misbehaviour at a meeting.

2. *Application of Act, and consequential provisions.* – (1) This Act shall apply to the bodies specified in the Schedule to this Act, and to such bodies as may for the time being be added to that Schedule by order made under subsection (3) below; and where this Act applies to a body, the foregoing section shall apply in relation to any committee of the body whose members consist of or include all members of the body, as that section applies in relation to the body itself, but so that for the purposes of paragraph (c) or subsection (4) of that section premises belonging to the body shall be treated as belonging to the committee.

(2) In the Schedule to the Defamation Act, 1952 (by virtue of which, among other things, newspaper reports of all proceedings at meetings of local authorities and their committees are privileged unless admission to the meeting is denied to representatives of newspapers and other members of the public), in the definition of 'local authority' in paragraph 13 for the reference to the Local Authorities (Admission of the Press to Meetings) Act, 1908, there shall be substituted a reference to this Act.

(3) Any body established by or under any Act may be added to the Schedule to this Act, and any body so added may be removed from the Schedule, by order of the appropriate Minister made by statutory instrument, but a statutory instrument made by a Minister under this section shall be of no effect unless it is approved by resolution of each House of Parliament; and for this purpose the appropriate Minister is, in the case of any body, the Minister of the Crown in charge of the Government department concerned or primarily concerned with the matters dealt with by that body, but an order made under this subsection by any Minister of the Crown shall be effective, whether or not he is the appropriate Minister.

3. *Short title, repeal, extent and commencement.* – (1) This Act may be cited as the Public Bodies (Admission to Meetings) Act, 1960.

(2) The Local Authorities (Admission of the Press to Meetings) Act, 1908, sub-paragraph (4) of paragraph 1

of Part IV of the Third Schedule to the Local Government Act, 1933, and section eighty-four of the Education (Scotland) Act, 1946, are hereby repealed.

(3) This Act shall not extend to Northern Ireland.

(4) This Act shall come into force on the first day of June, nineteen hundred and sixty-one.

SCHEDULE

Bodies To Which This Act Applies

1. The bodies to which in England and Wales this Act applies are –

(a) local authorities within the meaning of the Local Government Act, 1933, or the London Government Act, 1939, the Common Council of the City of London and the Council of the Isles of Scilly, and joint boards or joint committees constituted to discharge functions of any two or more of those bodies;

(b) the parish meetings of rural parishes;

(c) the Metropolitan Water Board, and joint boards and joint committees constituted by or under any Act for the purposes of water supply, and consisting of or including representatives of local authorities within the meaning of the Local Government Act, 1933;

(d) education committees (including joint education committees) constituted under Part II, and divisional executives constituted under Part III of the First Schedule to the Education Act, 1944;

(e) bodies constituted in accordance with regulations made under subsection (4) of section twenty-two of the National Health Service Act, 1946;

(f) regional hospital boards constituted under section eleven of the said Act of 1946;

(g) executive councils constituted under section thirty-one of the said Act of 1946, but only so far as regards the exercise of their executive functions;

(h) bodies not mentioned above but having, within the meaning of the Public Works Loans Act, 1875, power to levy a rate (other than police authorities).

APPENDIX 3.

LOCAL GOVERNMENT ACT, 1933, Sch. 3, Part IV, para. 1.

PART IV

Parish Councils

1. Days of meetings. – (1) A parish council shall in every year hold an annual meeting and at least three other meetings.

(2) The annual meeting of a parish council shall be held on or within fourteen days after the twentieth day of May in every year.

(3) The first meeting of a parish council constituted after the commencement of this Act shall be convened by the chairman of the parish meeting at which the first parish councillors are nominated.

(4) A meeting of a parish council shall be open to the public, unless the council otherwise direct.

(5) A meeting of a parish council shall not be held in premises licensed for the sale of intoxicating liquor, except in cases where no other suitable room is available for such meeting, either free of charge or at a reasonable cost.

APPENDIX 4.

MINISTRY OF HOUSING AND LOCAL GOVERNMENT CIRCULAR NO. 21/61

17*th May*, 1961.

Sir,

PUBLIC BODIES (ADMISSION TO MEETINGS) ACT, 1960

1. I am directed by the Minister of Housing and Local Government to draw your attention to the Public Bodies (Admission to Meetings) Act, 1960, which will come into operation on 1st June, 1961. The Act replaces the Local Authorities (Admission of the Press to Meetings) Act, 1908. It applies to a number of different types of public authority; this circular is concerned solely with its application to local authorities. The principal changes that it effects in the law are explained in Appendix I,* which contains a commentary on the provisions of the Act, Appendix II* lists changes in standing orders which the Minister now recommends, pending the completion of a general review of the model standing orders which is now in hand.

Relations with public and press

2. The Act deals with one aspect of local authorities' relations with public and press: namely, the right of the public to hear and of the press to report council meetings and the meetings of certain committees occupying a special position. The Minister has taken the opportunity to consult with the associations of local authorities on the more general question of public relations, with particular reference to relations with the press, and the following paragraphs set out certain principles which the Minister considers that local authorities should observe in their approach to these questions. The local authority associations agree generally with these views.

3. It is important for the health of local government that the public should be able to obtain regular information and informed objective comment about the day-to-day work of the local authorities. Because most people get their information about local authorities' business from their local newspapers, the relationship between the authorities and the press is of special importance. Both have a part to play. This circular is necessarily concerned only with the part of the local authorities.

4. The Minister is aware that most local authorities are alive to their responsibilities in these matters and, in particular, have arrangements with the local press which are satisfactory to both sides. He has no desire to suggest that practices which are working satisfactorily should be changed. Still less does he wish to propose any standard practices for adoption by all local authorities. Such authorities are responsible bodies and must make the arrangements which their experience suggests are most suitable for their own circumstances. The Minister asks only that every authority should make certain that it has satisfactory arrangements ensuring, so far as it is able to do so, that the public will be informed of what goes on, will be enabled to understand how the ratepayers'

money is spent, and will have the opportunity to form and express an informed public opinion. It is not merely a question of letting people know what their local authority have done and why; informed public opinion should have an opportunity of playing its part in the formation of policy. Minority voices should have the chance of expression.

5. While the particular methods adopted for keeping the press informed about local authority business can only be settled locally in the light of the way in which the particular local authority conducts its business, it is important that the local press should have a clear understanding of the reasons which lie behind the particular choice of methods, and that full consideration should be given to any views they may express in the matter.

6. Local authorities are executive as well as deliberative bodies. They frequently have business to transact and decisions to take where it would be inadvisable that premature publicity should be given to their proceedings. Their deliberations sometimes concern the private affairs of individuals which it would be against the public interest to publish. In the formative stages of some of their business free and uninhibited discussion might well be impeded if conducted in public. These reasons can be advanced to justify the conduct of a part of a local authority's business in private. They do not justify practices which result in the conduct of almost all the authority's business in private. Matters of real importance to the locality ought to be openly debated, unless there are compelling reasons against publicity. Council meetings should not, as occasionally occurs, be merely formal proceedings in which proposals formulated and discussed in private are rubber-stamped without debate.

7. If councils are to devote their attention to the really significant matters, much detailed business will necessarily be done by committees, often under delegated authority. Subject to the wider consideration of public interest which may sometimes make publicity undesirable, the public are entitled to know what decisions are taken in their name by a committee as well as by the council. How best to secure this will depend very much on the way in which the local authority's business is organised. Some authorities of all types and sizes already admit the press to the meetings of at any rate their main committees. There is nothing in the Act to prevent this and the practice is of particular value where committees exercise delegated powers. Some other councils may now find that this arrangement provides the answer for them too. Elsewhere, full reports to the council made available to the press, including reports of the action taken under delegated authority, or the regular supply of information to the press by press conferences or hand-outs, may be enough. Widely varying practices have been found satisfactory by the press; the important thing is that the public, and the press as an organ of communication to the public, should know how the local authority business is transacted and have the opportunity to find out what is going on.

8. Where a committee consists of or includes all the members of a local authority, the Act applies to meetings of that committee as it does to meetings of the council; the public and press may be excluded only on a resolution that certain business should, for stated reasons, be transacted in private. With such committees there is a particular likelihood that matters which ought to be openly debated will not be discussed in the council, and this provision secures that the public and press shall have an opportunity of being present when the main discussion takes place. It has been brought to the Minister's notice that a few authorities, accustomed to committees consisting of all council members, might, if they wish the committees to meet in private, decide to meet the situation created by the

Act by merely dropping one or two members. The Minister recognises that for the small authorities committees consisting of all or nearly all the members of the council may be the only convenient way to transact business; and that some of these committees may deal with matters which have to be discussed in private. In such a situation a reduction of the committees by one or two members might be the sensible arrangement. But what matters here is the nature of the business to be transacted. It would be quite wrong to use this device merely to defeat the purpose of the Act, and the Minister asks any authority which uses it to make sure that it does not result in the public and press being excluded from discussion of matters which ought to be openly debated.

9. Where business of a meeting normally open to the press and public is transacted in private, it is in the interests of good public relations that a clear indication should, wherever possible, be given of the reasons why it is considered that publicity would be prejudicial to the public interest. Only in exceptional cases, where an indication of the nature of the business would in itself be prejudicial to the public interest, should the explanation be simply in terms that the business is confidential.

10. Where the press are admitted to a meeting they should be able to obtain advance information about the business to be discussed. Newspapers and news agencies are entitled to receive copies of the agenda of meetings of the bodies to which the Act applies. The agenda itself may not be sufficient to explain the nature of the business to be discussed; a mere statement that the council will consider the report of (say) the general purposes committee would be of no help. In these circumstances (and providing the item is not one likely to be considered in private) the agenda should be accompanied by some further explanation. In many cases it would be possible to let the press have the actual committee reports as they are circulated to council members, and, unless these documents contain information which is confidential in the public interest, this is likely to be the most satisfactory course. If a separate statement has to be prepared, however, it should be drafted in such a way as to give the fullest help possible to anyone wanting to know both in advance and at the meeting what issues are before the council. The convenient course may well be for the documents to be sent to the press at the same time as to members, but in any event the press should receive them in good time and there should be no embargo to prevent them reporting and commenting on documents sent in this way before a council meeting. Where reporters are admitted to committee meetings, they should have advance copies of the agenda and other documents for these too.

Publicity for certain planning applications

11. The Minister has received a good many representations about the desirability of arranging for greater publicity for planning applications; and he asks local planning authorities to review their present arrangements in the light of the following comments.

12. Some people would like to see specific provision made for advertisement of all planning applications of any importance before decision is taken. The Minister does not believe that that would be right; it would in any event be bound seriously to increase delays, at a time when the great need is to speed up decisions. Planning applications are registered, and arrangements are already in force which secure publicity for many of them: under the Town and Country Planning Act, 1959, certain types of proposal relating to uses which may be particularly objectionable neighbours have to be advertised: substantial departures from the development plan are also given publicity in appropriate cases: and there

is publicity again when public inquiries are held by the Minister in connection with planning appeals and other planning procedures.

13. But there are some planning applications not covered by these arrangements where, in the Minister's view, there is scope for greater publicity than at present. The applications which the Minister has in mind are those which, if carried out, would affect the whole of a neighbourhood and which are therefore of considerable interest to a good many people. These cases are, in any given planning area, not very numerous. Nor can they be satisfactorily defined in any legal instrument. It is a question of judging whether a particular proposal is of such interest to a considerable part of the community that it ought to be made publicly known, whether by direct notification to persons affected or by local publicity or both, and an opportunity given for anyone concerned to make his views known before a decision is taken.

14. The Minister is aware that some authorities already go beyond their statutory obligations and when dealing with proposals publicise them and notify neighbours and others likely to be concerned, including local civic or amenity societies; but he would ask all authorities to consider whether enough is being done under their existing arrangements to secure appropriate publicity in cases of wide general interest.

15. Local planning authorities will still have to judge applications by principles which may not reflect the popular view in the immediate locality. Room has to be found for many developments which are not welcome neighbours. Permission often has to be given for some types of development, such as close-knit layouts of houses and flats in high blocks, which, however well-designed, are apt to cause local objection as being likely to change the character of the neighbourhood or to affect familiar views. Even so, it may well be in the best interests of planning to enable local opinion to declare itself before any decision is taken.

Conclusion

16. The essential thing in all these matters is that local authorities should keep the public and the press fully informed, and should enable themselves to take account of public opinion in reaching their decisions. They may sometimes have to take unpopular decisions, even decisions to which there is strong local opposition. It is the more important that they should be seen to have acted in the knowledge of public opinion and that their reasons for their actions should be fully understood.

I am, Sir,

Your obedient Servant,

E. A. SHARP

*Not reproduced in this Appendix.

APPENDIX 5.

LOCAL AUTHORITIES KNOWN TO ADMIT THE PRESS TO SOME OR ALL MAJOR COMMITTEES

Counties

Breconshire
Buckinghamshire
Devonshire
Glamorgan
Hampshire
Kent
East Suffolk
West Suffolk
Worcestershire

County Boroughs

Bath
Bolton
Bradford
Bristol
Cardiff
Exeter
Exeter
Gateshead
Great Yarmouth
Grimsby
Newcastle upon Tyne
Newport (Mon)
Norwich, Nottingham
Portsmouth
Salford
Swansea

London Boroughs

Bexley
Bromley
Ealing
Hackney
Haringey
Havering

Non-County Boroughs

Aberystwyth
Abingdon
Aldershot
Bewdley
Cardigan
Colne
Colwyn Bay
Dartmouth
Ilkeston
Lampeter
Monmouth
Mossley
Newbury
Newcastle under Lyme
New Windsor
Shrewsbury

Darwen
Ellesmere Port
Gravesend
Stafford
Tewkesbury
Yeovil

Urban Districts

Aberaeron
Adlington
Aldridge-Brownhills
Alfreton
Biddulph
Bognor Regis
Brixham
Budleigh Salterton
Chadderton
Cheshunt
Darton
Dodworth
Epping
Haltemprice
Hazel Grove & Bramhall
Horbury
Kearsley
Kidsgrove
Little Lever
Maltby
March
Marple
Mountain Ash
New Quay
Newton le Willows
Northfleet
Oakengates
Old Fletton
Oswaldtwistle
Potters Bar
Rawmarsh
Rickmansworth
Ripley
Stroud
Sunbury
Swanscombe
Thornton Cleveleys
Thurrock
Waltham Holy Cross
Westhoughton
Whitby
Whitfield
Whitstable

Rural Districts

Aberaeron
Aberystwyth
Bradfield
Cheadle
Cookham
Isle of Wight
Kiveton Park
Lancaster
Ludlow
Malling
Newcastle under Lyme
Oswestry
St. Neots
Teifiside
Tregaron
Wisbech

(Notes: Some of the smaller authorities have all members of

the council on their committees and therefore have, by law, to open their committees.

There is no central register of authorities with open committee meetings and authorities have, of course, the option, hence the above list is not comprehensive and is liable to change.

There is a wide divergence among the above authorities; some have all their committees open, others have only two or three major committees.

The above list is not definitive but gives examples of those authorities who do admit the Press to meetings.)

APPENDIX 6

TABLES

SURVEY RESULTS FOR COMMITTEE ON MANAGEMENT OF LOCAL GOVERNMENT AND ROYAL COMMISSION ON LOCAL GOVERNMENT IN ENGLAND

Table 1

Admission of the Press to Committee Meetings (other than Education Committee)

Population Range (thousands)	Total Authorities	Number of Authorities Admitting the Press to Meetings of: Committees			Sub-committees		
		All	Some	None	All	Some	None[1]
Counties							
10– 20 . .	1	–	1	–	–	1	–
20– 30 . .	1	–	–	1	–	–	1
30– 60 . .	5	1	2	2	1	–	4
60–100 . .	2	–	2	–	–	–	2
100–200 . .	9	–	9	–	–	1	8
200–400 . .	11	1	5	5	–	1	10
400–600 . .	14	–	6	8	–	–	14
Over 600 . .	12	–	7	5	–	2	10
All	55	2	32	21	1	5	49
County Boroughs							
30– 60 . .	6	1	5	–	1	2	3
60–100 . .	27	–	16	11	–	4	23
100–200 . .	29	–	16	13	–	7	22
200–400 . .	10	–	6	4	–	2	8
400–600 . .	3	1	–	2	–	1	2
Over 600 . .	3	–	3	–	–	1	2
All	78	2	46	30	1	17	60

Table 1 (cont.)

Population Range (thousands)	Total Authorities	Number of Authorities Admitting the Press to Meetings of: Committees			Sub-committees		
		All	Some	None	All	Some	None[1]
Non-County Boroughs							
Under 10 . .	64	11	21	32	1	–	42
10– 20 . .	47	9	18	20	–	2	43
20– 30 . .	28	5	10	13	–	2	25
30– 60 . .	83	4	41	38	–	7	75
60–100 . .	22	3	9	10	–	2	20
All	244	32	99	113	1	13	205
Urban Districts							
Under 10	65	2	19	34	–	1	41
10– 20 . .	50	7	19	24	1	1	39
20– 30 . .	20	3	10	7	–	1	15
30– 60 . .	16	2	6	8	–	1	14
60–100 . .	3	–	1	2	1	–	2
100–200 . .	2	–	1	1	–	–	2
All	156	24	56	76	2	4	113
Rural Districts							
Under 10 . .	35	3	13	19	–	–	24
10– 20 . .	55	4	20	31	–	–	45
20– 30 . .	31	–	8	23	–	–	23
30– 60 . .	24	1	6	17	–	–	22
60–100 . .	5	–	3	2	–	–	5
100–200 . .	1	–	1	–	–	–	1
All	151	8	51	92	–		120

[1] Authorities which do not appoint sub-committees have been excluded from these figures.

(Table 1. Report of Committee on Management of Local Government, Vol. 5)

Table 2

Availability of Council Agendas to the Press

Population Range (thousands)	Total Authorities	Number of Authorities: Making agendas available at least one clear day before meetings	Permitting press comment on agendas before meetings
Counties			
10– 20	1	1	1
20– 30	1	1	–
30– 60	5	5	3
60–100	2	2	1
100–200	9	9	7
200–400	11	11	9
400–600	14	14	11
Over 600	12	12	11
All	55	55	43
County Boroughs			
30– 60	6	6	4
60–100	27	26	23
100–200	29	28	28
200–400	10	10	10
400–600	3	3	3
Over 600	3	3	2
All	78	76	70
Non-County Boroughs			
Under 10	64	60	34
10– 20	47	47	29
20– 30	28	28	16
30– 60	83	79	61
60–100	22	22	18
All	244	236	158
Urban Districts			
Under 10	65	63	25
10– 20	50	49	32
20– 30	20	20	8
30– 60	16	12	11
60–100	3	3	3
100–200	2	2	1
All	156	149	80

(Table 2. Report of Committee on Management of Local Government, Vol. 5)

Table 2 (cont.)

Population Range (thousands)	Total Authorities	Number of Authorities: Making agendas available at least one clear day before meetings	Number of Authorities: Permitting press comment on agendas before meetings
Rural Districts			
Under 10 . .	35	31	17
10– 20 . .	55	54	26
20– 30 . .	31	29	13
30– 60 . .	24	22	15
60–100 . .	5	5	5
100–200 . .	1	1	1
All	151	142	77

Table 3

Approximate Average Attendance of Members of the Public at Council Meetings

(Excluding school children and other organised parties)

Population Range (thousands)	Total Authorities	Public Attendance: Average	Public Attendance: Range	Number of Authorities indicating nil attendance
Counties				
10– 20	1	–	–	1
20– 30	1	4	–	–
30– 60	5	2	0– 3	2
60–100	2	4	2– 6	–
100–200	9	1	0– 3	4
200–400	11	7	1–20	–
400–600	14	6	0–12	1
Over 600	12	7	2–15	–
All	55	–		8

(Table 3. Report of Committee on Management of Local Government, Vol. 5)

Table 3 (cont.)

Population Range (thousands)		Total Authorities	Public Attendance		Number of Authorities indicating nil attendance
			Average	Range	
County Boroughs					
30– 60		6	7	0–12	1
60–100		27	13	2–25	–
100–200		29	16	4–50	–
200–400		10	16	0–40	1
400–600		3	43	10–60	–
Over 600		3	25	20–30	–
	All	78	–		2
Non-County Boroughs					
Under 10		64	4	0–15	14
10– 20		47	7	0–30	7
20– 30		28	8	1–24	–
30– 60		83	10	0–30	2
60–100		22	17	0–50	1
	All	244	–		24
Urban Districts					
Under 10		65	4	0–20	15
10– 20		50	5	0–40	7
20– 30		20	6	0–20	3
30– 60		16	7	0–25	2
60–100		3	10	0–20	1
100–200		2	16	6–25	–
	All	156	–		28
Rural Districts					
Under 10		35	*	0–12	30
10– 20		55	*	0– 5	39
20– 30		31	*	0– 3	25
30– 60		24	1	0– 3	12
60–100		5	2	0– 5	2
100–200		1	0	–	1
	All	151	–		109

*Indicates less than one.

Table 4

Quantity of Council and Committee Papers Circulated to 'Average' member in a typical month

Population Range (thousands)	Total Authorities	No. of sides of typewritten foolscap or equiv. Excluding Education		Education only[1]	
		Average	Range	Average	Range
Counties					
10– 20 . .	1	92	–	57	–
20– 30 . .	1	80	–	46	–
30– 60 . .	5	150	24–368	77	15–186
60–100 . .	2	78	70– 85	85	30–140
100–200 . .	9	119	15–290	70	19–200
200–400 . .	11	126	60–171	67	5–155
400–600 . .	14	133(†2)	30–292	85	25–180
Over 600 . .	12	231	60–595	246	90–500
All	55	–	–	–	–
County Boroughs					
30– 60 . .	6	110	8–200	44	6–110
60–100 . .	27	113(†1)	20–275	53(†2)	3–195
100–200 . .	29	148(†1)	40–350	63(†1)	10–178
200–400 . .	10	184(†1)	100–450	82(†2)	20–130
400–600 . .	3	407	200–520	85	70–100
Over 600 . .	3	642	225–1,000	300	150–400
All	78	–	–	–	–
Non-County Boroughs					
Under 10 . .	64	35	6– 80	N/A	–
10– 20 . .	47	60(†1)	17–150	N/A	–
20– 30 . .	28	75	15–178	N/A	–
30– 60 . .	83(‡7)	112	16–420	31	6– 60
60–100 . .	22(‡19)	150	12–410	34	12– 65
All	244	–	–	–	–
Urban Districts					
Under 10 . .	65	28	5– 60	N/A	–
10– 20 . .	50	62	4–210	N/A	–
20– 30 . .	20	81	12–200	N/A	–
30– 60 . .	16	110(†1)	27–200	N/A	–
60–100 . .	3(‡1)	162	125–210	30	–
100–200 . .	2(‡1)	295	240–350	120	–
All	156	–	–	–	–

(Table 4. Report of Committee on Management of Local Government, Vol. 5)

Table 4 (cont.)

Population Range (thousands)	Total Authorities	No. of sides of typewritten foolscap or equiv. Excluding Education		Education only[1]	
		Average	Range	Average	Range
Rural Districts					
Under 10 . .	35(‡1)	25(†1)	4– 80	18	–
10– 20 . .	55	51(†1)	16–110	N/A	–
20– 30 . .	31	57	12–125	N/A	–
30– 60 . .	24	104	10–204	N/A	–
60–100 . .	5	151	50–221	N/A	–
100–200 . .	1	130	–	N/A	–
All	151	–	–	–	–

[1] Papers of education committee, sub-committees and governing/managing bodies.
‡Indicates the number of second-tier authorities in group having education committees.
†Indicates the number of authorities in group not supplying information.
N/A Indicates not applicable.

Table 5

LONDON BOROUGHS

Admission of the Press to Committee Meetings (other than Education Committee)

	Number of Authorities admitting press to meetings of Committees			Sub-committees		
	All	Some	None	All	Some	None
Inner London . .	–	–	12	–	2	10
Outer London . .	1	4	14	–	1	18
	1	4	26	–	3	28

(Table La. Report of Committee on Management of Local Government, Vol. 5)

Table 6
LONDON BOROUGHS
Availability of Council Agendas to the Press

	Total	Making agendas available at least one clear day before meetings	Permitting press comment on agendas before meeting
	Number of Authorities		
Inner London . .	12	12	12
Outer London. .	19	19	16
	31	31	28

(Table LIa. Report of Committee on Management of Local Government, Vol. 5)

Table 7
LONDON BOROUGHS
Quantity of Council and Committee papers circulated to 'Average' member in a typical month

	Number of Authorities	Number of sides of typewritten foolscap or equivalent			
		Excluding Education		Education only[1]	
		Average	Range	Average	Range
Inner London . .	12	167	66– 320	Not applicable	
Outer London . .	19	430	66–1,000	129	30–275

[1] Papers of educating committees, sub-committees and governing and managing bodies.

(Table XXIIIa. Report of Committee on Management of Local Government, Vol. 5)

Table 9

Regular readership of local newspapers, by type and size of local authority

		C.B.				M.B./U.D.					R.D.
	All informants 2199	*Total* 751	*Conur-bation* 294	250,000+ 206	60,000–250,000 251	*Total* 910	*Conur-bation* 113	60,000–100,000 235*	30,000–60,000 288	*Up to* 30,000 417	*Total* 538
	%	%	%	%	%	%	%	%	%	%	%
Regularly read at least 1 local newspaper	87	85	85	82	86	88	88	81	90	88	86
Regularly read 2 or more local newspapers	36	26	31	18	25	41	53	30	40	39	41

*Including supplementary sample

(Table 68. Royal Commission on Local Government in England; Research Study No. 9)

Table 8

LONDON BOROUGHS

Approximate average attendance of members of the public at Council Meetings

	Number of Authorities	Public Attendance	
		Average	Range
Inner London . .	12	16	6–30
Outer London . .	19	23	6–50

(Table XLIXa. Report of the Committee on Local Government, Vol. 5)

Table 10

Proportion of informants who regularly read each type of local newspaper

(*see also Table 22*)

Base (*all informants*)	2199
	%
Morning	10
Evening	50
Sunday	3
Weekly/fortnightly/monthly	55

(Adds to more than 100% due to multiple response)

(Table 69. Royal Commission on Local Government in England, Research Study No. 9)

Table 11

Number of local newspapers read regularly (1)

Base (*all informants*)	2199
	%
None	13
One	51
Two	28
Three	7
Four or more	1

(Table 70. Royal Commission on Local Government in England, Research Study No. 9)

Table 12

Number of local newspapers read regularly (2)

	Informants		*Socio-economic status*						*Education*		
	with a "home" area	*without a "home" area*	*Group* 1	2	3	4	5	*Never employed/ others*	*Higher*	*Second-ary*	*Lower*
(*Base*)	1710	484	97	168	773	477	531	153	129	448	1622
	%	%	%	%	%	%	%	%	%	%	%
None	12	17	10	8	13	14	15	16	12	10	14
One	51	52	52	48	51	50	51	56	44	52	51
Two	28	27	26	33	29	29	26	24	33	29	28
Three	7	4	11	9	6	6	7	4	10	8	6
Four or more	2	–	1	2	1	1	1	–	1	1	1

*Q.N.A.: 5 informants.

(Table 71. Royal Commission on Local Government in England, Research Study No. 9)

Table 13

Councillors' beliefs (1)

	Age		
	Under 45	45–64	65 or over
	%	%	%
Proportion of councillors believing that:			
The public does not know enough to make good use of existing council services	79	62	44
The public does not know enough to get a balanced picture of the way council conducts its affairs . . .	92	82	65
The public does not know enough to vote in an informed way . . .	54	52	35

(Page 231, Report of Committee on Management of Local Government, Vol. 2)

Table 14

Councillors' beliefs (2)

	Education		
	Elementary	Secondary	Further
	%	%	%
Proportion of councillors believing that:			
The public does not know enough to make good use of existing council services	60	57	77
The public does not know enough to get a balanced picture of the way council conducts its affairs . . .	76	82	91
The public does not know enough to vote in an informed way . . .	39	52	67

(Page 231, Report of Committee on Management of Local Government, Vol. 2)

Table 15

One thing which could be done to raise the level of public interest in local government activities—by council type

	All councils	Counties	County boroughs	Metropolitan boroughs	Municipal boroughs & urban districts	Rural districts
	%	%	%	%	%	%
Better coverage in press	15	15	16	7	13	18
Establish public relations organisations	14	16	22	17	16	8
Publicity organised by councillors themselves	12	11	13	21	13	12
Encouraging/ensuring public attendance at council meetings..	10	5	6	7	12	10
Education in schools	8	10	10	2	7	8
Making voting compulsory	6	5	11	7	9	1
Better radio/TV coverage	3	9	2	9	1	3
Extending power of local authority ..	2	2	1	4	2	2
Don't know: 'God knows' 'while they get what they want they don't take any notice', etc.	21	19	12	17	17	29
Other answers ..	8	6	6	9	9	8
Not answered ..	1	2	1	—	1	1
Total ..	100	100	100	100	100	100
(Numbers)	(1,235)	(152)	(134)	(46)	(483)	(420)

(Table 8.16. Report of Committee on Management of Local Government, Vol. 2)

Table 16

Informants hearing news of local council activities in the last month—by council type

	Informants living in:					
	County boroughs	Metro-politan boroughs	Municipal boroughs	Urban districts	Rural districts	All Informants
	%	%	%	%	%	%
'Have you heard anything that the council has done in the last month?'						
Yes	33	22	34	30	21	30
No	66	77	65	69	77	69
Don't know* ..	1	1	1	1	2	1
Total	100%	100%	100%	100%	100%	100%
% Base.	629	131	540	448	436	2,184

*Includes 3 people who gave no answer.

(Table 32. Report of the Committee on Management of Local Government, Vol. 3)

Table 17

Informants hearing news of local council activities in the last month—by sex and age

	Sex		Age				
	Male	Female	21–34	35–44	45–54	55–64	65 or more
	%	%	%	%	%	%	%
Heard news in last month	34	26	24	35	31	30	29
% Base	989	1,195	489	438	473	412	351

(Table 33. Report of the Committee on Management of Local Government, Vol. 3)

Table 18

Source of information of local news item most recently heard

	%
From the local papers	68
'By word of mouth' from friends, relatives, neighbours, or workmates ..	11
Saw the work (building, road mending, etc.) taking place	4
Heard from a councillor or the council office	4
From pamphlets or leaflets..	2
From the national press..	2
From meetings, lectures or talks	2
On television or radio	1
Other answers	5
Don't know	1
Total	100%
% Base*	645

*Those who had heard any news of their local council in the last month

(Table 36. Report of the Committee on Management of Local Government, Vol. 3)

Table 19

Informants reading a local council news item in the local press in the last month–by council type

	County boroughs	Metropolitan boroughs	Municipal boroughs	Urban districts	Rural districts	All Informants
	%	%	%	%	%	%
Read local council news in local press last month	25	8	24	19	13	20
% Base ..	629	131	540	448	436	2,184

(Table 37. Report of the Committee on Management of Local Government, Vol. 3)

Table 20

Informants reading any local papers—by council type

	Informants living in:					
	County boroughs	Metro-politan boroughs	Municipal boroughs	Urban districts	Rural districts	All Infor-mants
	%	%	%	%	%	%
Informants reading local papers:						
Regularly*	84	53	78	76	83	79
Not regularly	8	23	13	11	6	10
Not within the last 12 months†	8	24	9	13	11	11
Total	100%	100%	100%	100%	100%	100%
% Base	629	131	540	448	436	2,184

*Regularly = two out of the last three issues.

†Includes a small number (1% of the total) who gave no answer.

(Table 38. Report of the Committee on Management of Local Government, Vol. 3)

Table 21

Informants reading any local papers—by age of informant

	21–34	35–54	55–64	65 or more	All Infor-mants
	%	%	%	%	%
Informants reading local newspapers:					
Regularly*	73	80	83	80	79
Not regularly	16	10	7	5	10
Not within the last 12 months*	11	10	10	15	11
Total	100%	100%	100%	100%	100%
% Base	489	911	412	351	2,184†

*The notes given in table 20 apply here.

†21 informants did not give their age and are included in the total figures only.

(Table 39. Report of the Committee on Management of Local Government, Vol. 3)

Table 22

Type of local paper read

(*See also Table 10*)

	Local Mornings	Local Evenings*	Local Sundays	Local Weeklies†
	%	%	%	%
Read this type regularly..	9	52	2	65
Don't read this type regularly ..	47	30	31	29
No such paper in area‡	44	18	67	6
Total	100%	100%	100%	100%
% Base (those who read a local paper regularly)	1,722	1,722	1,722	1,722

*Includes the London Evenings for people living in the G.L.C. area.

†Includes bi-weeklies and fortnightlies and the few papers distributed free of charge containing some local news and much local advertising.

‡No paper of this type served the local authority area in which the informant lives. The information was derived from interviewers, enquiries in the field plus reference to *The Newspaper Press Directory* (Benn Bros. 1965).

Note: Local papers produced in the larger provincial towns were considered to serve neighbouring authorities if they included local news of those authorities.

(Table 40. Report of the Committee on Management of Local Government, Vol. 3)

Table 23

Informants reading regularly

	%
(a) A local morning paper	7
(b) A local evening paper	41
(c) A local Sunday paper	2
(d) A local weekly, or bi-weekly or fortnightly paper	51
Total*..	101%
% Base	2,184

*Adds to more than 100% as some people read more than one type of paper.

(Table 41. Report of the Committee on Management of Local Government, Vol. 3)

Table 24

The number of local papers informants say they read regularly

	(I) Shown as proportions of all regular readers	(II) Shown as proportions of the whole electorate
None	*	21
One	67	53
Two	28	22
Three	4	3
Four†	1	1
Total	100%	100%
% Base ..	1,722	2,184

* Not applicable

† One informant said that he (or she) read five local papers regularly.

(Table 42. Report of the Committee on Management of Local Government, Vol. 3)

Table 25

Informants tuned in to radio or television programmes about local government in the last year

	T.V.	Radio
Informants saying they:		
(1) Have seen/heard programmes on local government in the last year	32	9
(2) Have tuned in to T.V. or radio but have not seen/heard programmes on local government*	62	78
X (3) Have not looked at T.V./listened to radio in the last year†	6	13
Total	100%	100%
% Base	2,184	2,184

*Includes a few people who did not know whether they had seen/heard a programme or not.

†Includes a few people who gave no answer.

(Table 43. Report of the Committee on Management of Local Government, Vol. 3)

Index